THE PARENT/ COMMUNITY Connection

IN THE CLASSROOM

Connecting your classroom to **parents**, **community**, and **character education**

JULIE L. GAINES

The Parent/Community Connection in the Classroom: Connecting your classroom to parents, community, and character education

Published by Character Development Group
PO Box 35136, Greensboro, NC 27425
Toll-Free 888-262-0572, Phone 336-668-9373, Fax 336-668-9375
www.CharacterEducation.com

Printed in the United States of America

ISBN 1-892056-43-7

ACKNOWLEDGEMENTS

A sincere thank you to the following:

- The staff and parents at Providence Spring Elementary for their support and encouragement.
- Betty Hensley for believing in the Parent Connection and persevering to make it happen.
- Julie Babb for her wisdom and for giving me the opportunity to share the Parent Connection with others.
- My sweet little characters Justin, Jared, and Jenna—I am blessed to be your Mom.
- My husband, Jeff—for his enduring love.

Table of Contents

Foreword

By now, all that we do in the area of character education is imitated, copied or adapted from something we have seen, heard or read about. The Charlotte-Mecklenburg School system received a federal grant that provided the opportunity for 25 pilot schools to attend conferences, bring in guest speakers and assist students with service learning projects. Part of the grant requires that these 25 schools share what they are doing. The ideas are never ending and always exciting. Providence Spring Elementary is one of the 25 pilot schools.

When Providence Spring opened in August 2002, staff from different schools came with many ideas for a character education initiative. We all agreed that to have our staff and students use the same "language" was of utmost importance. We further agreed that our initiative needed to to be worked into the curriculum. We needed someone to go into the classroom on a regular basis and use this character language. This would help our teachers be able to use the language in their daily lessons. I had just left Cotswold Elementary School, A National School of Character in 2000. At Cotswold, all support staff did lessons in the classrooms. This was an idea we wanted to copy but we did not have the number of support staff that Cotswold had. We decided to adapt and start a "parent connection." Mrs. Teresa Fletcher and I trained that first parent group using videos from Cotswold. Parents learned the language of character education and techniques for presenting in front of a class. Mrs. Julie Gaines was one of the first parents trained. Her enthusiasm was contagious. It was not long before her ideas were being shared in her neighborhood and in the parent center at school. She agreed to take over the training of our parents for the school year 2003-04. Our Parent Connection has been shared with many other schools. Mrs. Gaines has created materials that can be used by parent and community groups. Her training tips and ideas can help establish a strong connection in the classroom. You will find yourself imitating, copying or adapting. Enjoy the process!

"Remember that...
What you do as well as what you don't do
can make a difference.
The question is...
How much difference do you want to make?"
—Duane Hodgin

Betty Hensley
Co-Chair Character Education
Providence Spring Elementary

The Parent Connection

Parenting is complex, challenging and filled with opportunities for growth, not just for children! Many times you may have wished for a "Parenting 101" manual. Sometimes it is a relief to know that "trained educators" are responsible for your children's education; however, you want to be involved in your child's school. Perhaps you would you like to help children, your own and their peers, develop positive character. Don't you wish there was an accessible "How to be a Positive, Effective and Involved Parent" manual that would provide clearly written, tried and true recipes complete with all of the essential ingredients, including the preparation time and presentation ideas? Guess what? You have found the book! This "recipe," developed by Julie Gaines, has been tested many times and according to children, parents, teachers and administrators, the results are supreme!

Julie Gaines, a parent, and extraordinarily talented and generous volunteer, has harnessed her enthusiasm, energy and creative ideas to help parents and schools work together to promote positive character in students. Her passion will attract you immediately. Her experience, both in the workplace and as a volunteer in her children's school, helped Julie write this easy to use, highly successful manual. I think of it as the "How to be a Positive, Effective and Involved Parent" manual; however she has named it *The Parent/Community Connection in the Classroom*!

Monthly ideas developed for parents at Providence Spring Elementary, where Julie is a volunteer, include clear, detailed, interesting lessons that parents and community volunteers can teach each month. Julie Gaines understands your busy lifestyles, and the fact that many of you are not trained educators, therefore she makes sure that the lessons require only brief preparation (using materials usually found in most of our homes) and the actual lessons are taught in 30 minutes or less. Julie writes with clarity, passion and commitment. It is evident that she cares about the character development of children, her own and others, as well as the opportunity and the tools for parents to be involved. Each one of you cares about your child's character and hopes to be an actively involved partner in the school. Julie Gaines, a shining model of positive character and of parent involvement, makes it possible for you to contribute in a meaningful and manageable way. It is with joy and anticipation that we celebrate the publication of *The Parent/Community Connection in the Classroom*.

Julie Babb
Director of Character Development
Charlotte-Mecklenburg Schools
October 2005

Introduction

This book is intended to be used by parents and members of the community as a guide for teaching character education lessons in the classroom. The simple lesson outlines and corresponding activity ideas make teaching character lessons fun and easy. Recruiting your parents and community members (e.g., businesses, faith and youth organizations) to teach monthly 30-minute lessons will increase the effectiveness of your school's character education initiative. Everyone benefits—the home, school, and community—when basic core values are supported.

Each unit includes:
- An easy-to-follow outline for each character trait lesson.
- Book suggestions per grade level.
- Engaging activity ideas.

In addition, this book includes character skits, bulletin board ideas, and sample letters to parents with suggestions for ways to develop character at home.

The Parent and Community Connection is designed to promote a character education alliance between schools, parents, and the community. By working together we can increase awareness and gain the support and vision you need to enhance your initiative. In the words of a great visionary, Helen Keller: "Alone we can do so little; together we can do so much."

Getting Started

"Good character is contagious; pass it on."

—Author Unknown

**Here are the V.I.T.A.L. fundamentals for making
The Parent and Community Connection:**

Volunteer coordinator. Work with your PTA to designate a Character Education representative, or appoint a school staff member to coordinate your volunteers.

Invite parents or members of the business and faith community to be classroom character education volunteers at Meet the Teacher or Open House, through newsletters or parent information sent home at the beginning of the school year. Some volunteers may choose to alternate teaching monthly lessons with another volunteer in the class. This works fine, but encourage the volunteers to complete their first lesson together and explain to the students what they can expect throughout the school year. A maximum of two volunteers per classroom is best.

Teach your volunteers about the guidelines and expectations at an orientation meeting. You may want to offer this at two different times in order to accommodate more of your volunteers. (A sample orientation letter follows.)

At the first of each month, if your volunteers do not have their own books, provide them with a character trait information packet. This should include the lesson outline, available books, and activity suggestions.

Library for character education books and resources. Establish a location for volunteers to have easy access to the resources they will need for their lessons. Storybooks should be available and separated by trait and grade level. You may also want to offer additional props such as puppets and hats to enhance the character lessons. Consider limiting check-out of the materials to one hour. This will ensure availability for others. Also, encourage volunteers to select only books from their assigned grade level. This prevents students from hearing the same book year after year.

Sample Volunteer Orientation Letter

Dear Volunteer:

Thank you for volunteering to teach character education in your child's classroom.

Each month throughout the school year we highlight a different character trait. You will be responsible for teaching a monthly 30-minute lesson. This will include leading a discussion of the trait, reading a book to the students, and involving the class in an activity appropriate for their grade level.

At the beginning of each month, prepare your lesson with the materials provided. This includes a lesson outline for the trait, a list of books available in the character education library at our school, and activity ideas. If you choose to read a book or conduct an activity outside of those suggested, you are encouraged to review your plans with the classroom teacher ahead of time. In addition, you will need to contact your teacher at the first of each month and coordinate the day and time of your presentation.

Your commitment to support our character education initiative is greatly appreciated. By working together we can build strong character in our children that will last a lifetime.

"How wonderful it is that no one need wait a single moment before starting to improve the world."
—Anne Frank

RESPECT

TREAT OTHERS THE WAY YOU WANT TO BE TREATED!

**We may look different on the outside,
but we have the same feelings on the inside.**

Respect

"Respect is learned, earned, and returned."

—Author Unknown

Pre-teach: Introduce yourself and tell the students which trait you will be discussing today. Ask the following questions and call on different students for answers. Below each question are examples of the types of responses you are looking for. You may need to rephrase the students' answers or guide them along.

(Ask) **What does the word *respect* mean?**

1. Showing consideration for other people and their property.
2. Caring for ourselves, family, community, and school.
3. Appreciating and accepting individual differences.
4. Treating others the way that you would want to be treated.

(Ask) **How can you show respect?**

1. Use kind words and good manners.
2. Listen to what others have to say.
3. Follow the rules.
4. Appreciate differences among people.
5. Take care of other people's property at school, home, and in the community.
6. Help others.

Book: Read and discuss a book that teaches a lesson about respect. *(Book list follows.)*

(Ask) **How would you practice respect if...**

1. Someone on the school bus is saying unkind words and bullying another student. What should you do?
2. One of your classmates or siblings shares a story you have already heard many times before. How should you react?
3. The park is closed for construction and the sign says "Keep Out!" Your friends want to play anyway. What should you do? What if someone takes a marker and starts writing on the sign?
4. Your teacher brings in a very special souvenir from her vacation. She allows it to be passed around the classroom. How should you handle the special treasure? What if it gets broken?
5. What should you do if you see a classmate or teacher with their arms full struggling to open a door? Or you see them drop a stack of papers on the ground?
6. Your coach chooses another player to put in the game and you feel it should be you?

(Encourage students to come up with a few more situations to discuss together as a class.)

Activity: Complete an activity to go along with your lesson. *(Activity suggestions follow.)* You may choose to incorporate an activity into your lesson at any time. Often visuals and experiments are very effective at the beginning and will get your students excited about the lesson.

Closing comment: If you expect respect, then be the first to show it!

Read and discuss the quote at the beginning of this section and then give a bookmark to each student. (Bookmarks follow. Make copies as needed.)

Respect Activities

Reaching Out with Respect
(Suggested for all grades)
Materials: One sheet of paper

Practice firm handshakes in class with each other. Talk about how offering your hand and looking that person in the eye is a way to show respect. Discuss other ways our hands can show respect—applause, reaching out to help someone, putting our hand over our heart during the Pledge of Allegiance, handling delicate things with care, keeping our hands to ourselves, and cleaning up. Have students trace around their right hand on a piece of paper. On each finger have them write a way to show respect for others. Encourage students to share some of the statements they have written. If possible, display the hands in the room or hallway.

Simon Says: "Who Are You?" (Suggested for grades K-2)
Materials: None

Students play a variation of Simon Says that highlight their similarities and differences. The objective is to teach respect and tolerance for each other. Tell them to watch carefully as they play the game because at the end each student must tell one new thing they learned about a classmate. Begin the game like this:

Simon Says: "Everyone with brown eyes, stand up."
Simon Says: "Everyone who has a cat, put your right hand up."

Book Suggestions for Respect

Kindergarten
- *Arthur's Nose*, Marc Brown
- *The Grouchy Ladybug*, Eric Carle
- *The Ugly Caterpillar*, Eric Carle

First Grade
- *Arthur's Eyes*, Marc Brown
- *Dog Eared*, Amanda Harvey
- *William's Doll*, Charlotte Zolotow

Second Grade
- *Big Al*, Andrew Clements
- *Charlie the Caterpillar*, Dom Deluise
- *Enemy Pie*, Derek Munson

Third Grade
- *A Coat of Many Colors*, Dolly Parton
- *Nana Upstairs, Nana Downstairs*, Tomie dePaola
- *Old Henry*, Joan W. Blos

Fourth Grade
- *Moss Gown*, William Hooks
- *Annie and the Old One*, Miska Miles
- *It's a Spoon, Not a Shovel*, Caralyn Buchner

Fifth Grade
- *If a Bus Could Talk: The Rosa Parks Story*, Faith Ringgold
- *The Black Snowman*, Phil Mendez
- *Smokey Night*, Eve Bunting

Simon Says: "Everyone whose favorite sport is basketball, stand on one foot."
Simon Says: "Everyone who speaks more that one language, jump up and down."
Simon Says: "If you like to eat spinach, nod your head." And so on.

At the end of the game have students sit down in a circle. Ask each to student to share something new they learned about another student. Discuss respect for each others uniqueness and how to appreciate our differences. (www.education-world.com)

Out of My Mouth (Suggested for all grades)
Materials: You will need a tube of toothpaste and a paper plate.

The theme of this activity is to watch what you say because you can't take it back. Select a volunteer to come up to the front and ask them to squeeze all of the toothpaste out of the tube onto the plate. Ask another volunteer to come up front. Once your volunteer is in place, ask him or her to carefully put all of the toothpaste back into the tube. Soon the volunteer will give up and respond that it is impossible. Explain to the class that getting the toothpaste out was much easier that putting it back in. Our words can be just like that. Once they come out of our mouths, we can't put them back in. This is why we should always take care to use kind words and speak respectfully to others. Thoughtless, mean, and angry words really hurt. Remember: The toothpaste was caught on a plate so it would not make a mess. Unkind words can't be caught this way, and what we say can make a big mess. Always take care to use kind and respectful words. (*Object Talks For Any Day*, Kokmeyer)

It's Not Easy Being Green (Suggested for grades K-1)
Materials: Song or video of Kermit the Frog singing "It's Not Easy Being Green"

Play song or video for the students. Discuss what it means to be different and how it feels. For example, Are you short or tall? Do you or someone you know have a physical disability? How do people from other countries and those who speak a different language feel? Ask the students to identify ways they can demonstrate respect to those people who are different from them. (*Character Education*, Graham and McKoy)

We say, "Thank you."
We say, "Please."
We don't interrupt or tease.
We don't argue. We don't fuss.
We listen when folks talk to us.
We share our toys and take our turn.
Good manners aren't too hard to learn.
It's really easy, when you find
Good manners means...
Just being kind!

Manners Matter
(Suggested for grades 2-5)
Materials: Copy of poem at left

Talk about good manners and how they are an important way to demonstrate respect. Read the following poem to the students. (*If you do not have copies of the poem you can write it on the board.*) Have the students work in small groups to make a song or rap out of the poem. Select volunteers to present their version of the poem to the class.

Sweet Respect (Suggested for all grades)
Materials: Bowl of water, pepper, sugar, and a bar of soap

Begin by sprinkling pepper liberally on the water. Tell the students that the pepper represents the people around them—classmates, teachers, friends, and family. Discuss the fact that how we get along with people is largely determined by how we treat and speak to them. Our words can be very powerful tools, either for good or bad, and it's important to learn positive and respectful ways of speaking to others. Take the bar of soap and tell the students it represents unkind and hurtful language. *(Touch the bar of soap to the center of the water. The soap will repel the pepper and cause it to be dispersed to the side of the bowl.)* Tell students that when we speak unkindly to others, they will not want to be around us, and they will scatter just like the pepper. Take a teaspoon of sugar and pour it in the center of the water. Compare the sugar to the sweetness of kind and respectful words. *(The pepper will be drawn to the sugar.)* Tell the students that being respectful towards other people usually causes them to be drawn to us and want to be our friend. (*10-Minute Life Lessons for Kids*, Jamie Miller)

Race for Respect (Suggested for grades 2-5)
Materials: None

Divide the class into two groups. Assign Group 1 "Respect at Home" and Group 2 "Respect at School." Allow five minutes for each group to come up with as many ways as possible to show respect at their assigned place. When time is up have each group read their list to the class. The group with the most respectful actions WINS!

Role Play (Suggested for grades 2-5)
Materials: None

Divide the students into groups of 3-5 and ask each group to develop a short skit about respect. Each skit should show a student responding to a situation in a respectful manner. Have each group present its skit to the class.

Heart-ful Respect (Suggested for grades 2-5)
Materials: Hammer, nail, block of wood

Begin by striking the nail into the wood with the hammer. Explain to the students that this is what it feels like in a persons heart when they are teased, *(hit the nail again)* put-down, *(hit the nail)* excluded, *(hit the nail)* the victim of gossip or a cruel email etc. Next, remove the nail and say, "Even after 'I'm sorry' is said, *(show students the hole left by the nail)* a hole is left in that person's heart. Don't be the kind of person that hurts the hearts of others. Treat everyone with kindness and respect.

BOOKMARKS FOR RESPECT

"Respect is learned, earned, and returned." —Author Unknown

"Respect is learned, earned, and returned." —Author Unknown

"Respect is learned, earned, and returned." —Author Unknown

"Respect is learned, earned, and returned." —Author Unknown

"Respect is learned, earned, and returned." —Author Unknown

"Respect is learned, earned, and returned." —Author Unknown

"Respect is learned, earned, and returned." —Author Unknown

"Respect is learned, earned, and returned." —Author Unknown

"Respect is learned, earned, and returned." —Author Unknown

"Respect is learned, earned, and returned." —Author Unknown

(Make copies as needed.)

The Parent/Community Connection in the Classroom

RESPONSIBILITY

RESPONSIBILITY RULES!

YOU CAN COUNT ON ME!

CAN I COUNT ON YOU?

RESPONSIBILITY SERVED HERE

It all depends on me!

MR RESPONSIBILITY

Responsibility

"I am responsible for doing the work I need to do today even though it may be hard."

—Helen Keller

Pre-teach: Reacquaint yourself with the students and tell them which trait you will be discussing today. Ask the following questions and call on different students for answers. Below each question are examples of responses. You may need to rephrase students' answers or guide them along.

(Ask) What is *responsibility*?
1. Being accountable for what you do, in both your actions and behavior.
2. Doing the right thing at the right time, so others can trust and depend on you.

(Ask) What are ways you can show responsibility?
1. Complete your homework and chores on time without being reminded.
2. Follow through on your commitments, even when you don't feel like it.
3. Accept responsibility for your mistakes and learn from them. Don't make excuses or blame others.
4. Take care of your things and those of other people. Return items you borrow.
5. Find out what needs to be done and do it.
6. Make wise choices, such as choosing to eat healthy foods and wearing a helmet when biking.
7. Always do your very best. Others are counting on you!

Book: Read and discuss a book that teaches a lesson about responsibility. *(Book suggestions follow.)*

(Ask) How would you demonstrate responsibility if...
1. You broke the wheel off your brother's new skateboard?
2. Your friend asks you to play and you haven't finished your homework?
3. You're playing a really fun game at your friend's house and it's time to go home?
4. You promised your mom or dad you would clean your room but you just don't feel like it?
5. It is time to go to bed and you just remembered that your book report is due tomorrow?
6. You agreed to take care of your neighbor's dog while she is away, but now a friend has invited you to a sleepover?
7. Your mom is not feeling well and could really use some extra help around the house?
8. You forgot to bring your homework home from school, including the book you need to study for tomorrow's test?

(Ask) What are some other situations where we can demonstrate responsibility?
(Encourage students to come up with a few more situations to discuss together as a class.)

Activity: Complete an activity to go along with your lesson. *(Activity suggestions follow.)* You may choose to incorporate an activity into your lesson at any time. Often visuals and experiments are very effective at the beginning and will get your students excited about the lesson.

Closing comment: Remember only *you* have the ability to have responsibility. Be a person others can trust and count on to do the right thing! *(Pass out Responsibility bookmarks with the quote at the beginning of this section. Bookmarks follow. Make copies as needed.)*

Responsibility Activities

Responsi-*bill*-lity (Suggested for grades 2-5)
Materials: A dollar bill

Look what I brought with me today. *(Hold up the dollar bill for the students to see.)* All of us know how to spend money. Do we all need money? What do we use money for? *(Briefly discuss needs and wants.)* When I hold this dollar bill in my hand, it doesn't block my vision of the things around me. I can see my family, friends, people who might need help, and I can see work that needs to be done. The problem comes when I hold money so close to me *(hold dollar in front of your eyes)* that it's all I can see or care about. If I love money too much, that can lead to trouble. I might begin to make foolish and selfish purchases, thinking only of myself instead of making responsible choices and thinking about the needs of others. Having money is not a problem. But if I love money too much—and hold it too close—it becomes a problem. What are some good and responsible things we can do with money? *(Object Talks for Any Day, Kokmeyer)*

Responsibili-Tree (Suggested for grades K-3)
Materials: White, brown, and green construction paper. Tree trunk with branches and leaf stencils made from heavy cardboard

Book Suggestions for Responsibility

Kindergarten
Berenstain Bears Trouble at School, Jan Berenstain
Five Little Monkeys With Nothing To Do, Eileen Christelow
The Ant and the Grasshopper, Amy Lowry Poole

First Grade
Annie Shows Off, Shelagh Canning
Clean Your Room, Harvey Moon!, Pat Cummings
Pigsty, Mark Teague

Second Grade
Arthur's Pet Business, Marc Brown
Mrs. Katz and Tush, Patricia Polacco
Tops and Bottoms, Janet Stevens

Third Grade
A Day's Work, Eve Bunting
Betsy Who Cried Wolf, Gail Carson
Crow Boy, Taro Tashima

Fourth Grade
Horton Hatches the Egg, Dr. Seuss
The Paper Boy, Dave Pilkey
Your Job is Easy, Carl Sommer

Fifth Grade
Kate Shelley: Bound for a Legend, Robert D. San Souci
The Boy of the Three-Year Nap, Dianne Snyder
Why Do Mosquitos Buzz in People's Ears?, Verna Aardema

Give each student one piece each of the white, brown, and green construction paper. Instruct them to use the brown paper to trace and cut out the tree trunk and then glue it on their white paper. Then use the green paper to cut and trace out leaves and then glue the leaves on the branches of the tree trunk. Students will then write responsible actions that they will perform on each of the leaves (e.g., take out the garbage, feed the dog, set the table).

Play the "What if....?" Game (Suggested for grades K-3)

Materials: A sample lunch, for example, a sandwich, a piece of fruit, carton of milk

Ask the students a series of "What if...?" questions.

1. What if the farmer who grew the grain to make the bread for this sandwich decided to play ball instead of harvesting the grain? *(Explain that we wouldn't have any bread to eat, then take the bread off of the sandwich.)*
2. What if the farmer who raised the animals for the meat decided he was just too tired to take the animals to market? *(Take the meat away.)*
3. What if the dairy farmer decided it was too cold and rainy to go out and milk the cows in the morning? *(Take away the cheese and milk.)*
4. What if the workers who harvest fruits and vegetables were too busy watching TV to work in the fields? *(Take away any fruit and vegetables.)*
5. What if the store manager and employees at the grocery store didn't feel like working for a few weeks and played with friends instead? *(Take away everything else and explain that the store wouldn't be open and we could not get the things we need.)*
6. See what can happen when people do not show responsibility? We count on others to be responsible and do their job correctly and on time. The jobs that you have are just as important. *(Ask the students to give examples of their "jobs.")* When you do what is expected of you to the best of your ability, then you are being responsible and others can count on YOU! (www.charactercenter.com)

Responsibility Is My Bag! (Suggested for grades K-2)

Materials: Paper bag

Give everyone a lunch-sized paper bag. Tell the students how they can show responsibility by helping to keep their family car neat and tidy. Explain that they will decorate their bag. When they are finished, you will put a small hole near the top so the bag can be placed over a switch or knob in the car and used as a trash catcher. Tell the students it will be their responsibility to empty the bag when it's full and put it back in its place.
(Mom's Big Activity Book for Building Little Characters, Bertolini)

Sweet Responsibility (Suggested for grades 2-5)

Materials: Small apples and wrapped candy, enough so that you have one for each student

Show the students what you have. Ask them individually which of the two items they would like and let them take the one of their choice. First speak to those that chose the candy, saying something like, "You have chosen the food that will give you quick energy. It is very sweet and delicious to eat. However, it doesn't last very long and it is mostly empty calories. A few minutes after you eat it, you'll be hungry for more." To those who chose the apple say, "The apple will also give you energy and it is sweet to the taste. However, the apple is nutritious and will supply you with extra vitamins. You will feel more satisfied and benefit from the energy it gives for a longer period of time. The decision to take the apple was a very wise one. Now, ask the children how you can compare the apple and candy to our responsibilities and the choices we face every day. Many of the choices we make can bring us immediate pleasure but have no long-lasting value (like the candy) or a wise and responsible choice will bring us a longer-lasting type of happiness and satisfaction (like the apple).

Examples:
1. You are working on your homework when a friend calls and invites you to come over and watch a movie. Which choice will probably give immediate pleasure and which choice would give you long-term satisfaction? Which is the responsible choice?
2. You have been saving your money to buy a new skateboard, but as you walk by the arcade you think about spending the money to play a few arcade games.
3. You have the opportunity to finish your science project ahead of schedule or play basketball with your friends.

(*10-Minute Life Lessons for Kids*, Miller)

Role Play (Suggested for grades 4-5)
Materials: None

Divide the students into small groups and ask them to develop a skit about responsibility. Have each group present to the class. Be sure and discuss each skit after the students have finished and point out the responsible behavior.

A Symphony of Character (Suggested for all grades)
Materials: Musical instrument that you can play

Bring in your instrument and draw a line of music on the board with notes. Play the music as written. Next, erase several of the notes and replay the music. Notice how different the music sounds. Explain the importance of each note in the composition. They all have a purpose to make the music work. It can be beautiful and complete only when each note is doing its part. Each of us is like a note in a musical composition. When we do our part and take responsibility for our actions, then we can make beautiful "music" in our lives and for those around us.

BOOKMARKS FOR RESPONSIBILITY

> *"I am responsible for doing the work I need to do today even though it may be hard."*
> —Helen Keller

> *"I am responsible for doing the work I need to do today even though it may be hard."*
> —Helen Keller

> *"I am responsible for doing the work I need to do today even though it may be hard."*
> —Helen Keller

> *"I am responsible for doing the work I need to do today even though it may be hard."*
> —Helen Keller

> *"I am responsible for doing the work I need to do today even though it may be hard."*
> —Helen Keller

> *"I am responsible for doing the work I need to do today even though it may be hard."*
> —Helen Keller

> *"I am responsible for doing the work I need to do today even though it may be hard."*
> —Helen Keller

> *"I am responsible for doing the work I need to do today even though it may be hard."*
> —Helen Keller

> *"I am responsible for doing the work I need to do today even though it may be hard."*
> —Helen Keller

> *"I am responsible for doing the work I need to do today even though it may be hard."*
> —Helen Keller

(Make copies as needed.)

HONESTY

Honesty

"Honesty is always the best policy."
—George Washington

Pre-teach: Greet the students and briefly review the traits you have discussed on your previous visits. Tell the students that today you will be discussing the trait *honesty*. Ask the following questions and call on different students for answers. Below each question are examples of the type of responses you are looking for. You may need to rephrase the students' answers or guide them along.

(Ask) **What does *honesty* mean?**
1. To be truthful.
2. To not lie, cheat, or steal.

(Ask) **Why is honesty important?**
1. Honest people are trustworthy, dependable, and respected by others.
2. It is the right thing to do. It feels good.
3. Telling the truth lets everyone know what happened and keeps the wrong person from being blamed for something they didn't do.

(Ask) **What are the consequences of dishonesty?**
1. Losing the trust and respect of others.
2. The need to tell more lies in order to cover up.
3. You may face punishment and embarrassment.

(Ask) **What are the qualities of an honest person?**
1. Tells the truth, regardless of the consequence.
2. Admits when he or she is wrong.
3. Does not cheat or steal.
4. Does not exaggerate to make things seem different than they are.
5. Keeps promises and encourages others to be truthful

Book: Read and discuss a book that teaches a lesson about honesty. *(Book suggestions follow.)*

(Ask) **How can you demonstrate the trait honesty in the following situations?**
1. The cashier only charges you for two candy bars when you really bought three.
2. You find a $10 bill in the hallway at school, or in the sofa seat cushion at home.
3. A friend asks if he can copy your answers during a test.
4. You promised your mom or dad you would clean your room, but you watched TV instead.
5. You borrowed your friend's skateboard and lost it.

6. At the store, you see one of your friends put something in her pocket without paying for it.
7. You think no one will notice if you take two cookies from the tray when the sign says "One cookie per person."
8. The rule states that you must be 8 years old to play. Who will know that you're only 7 years old?

Activity: Complete an activity to go along with your lesson. *(Activity suggestions follow.)*

Concluding comment: Always tell the truth—it's the right thing to do. Your family and friends will respect you for it. *(Pass out Honesty bookmarks. Bookmarks follow. Make copies as needed.)*

Honesty Activities

Oh, What a Tangled Web We Weave!
(Suggested for grades 2-5)
Materials: Ball of yarn

Arrange ahead of time to have your child or another student help you with this demonstration. Secretly ask the child to give false answers to each question that you ask. This will begin after he or she has taken a seat in a chair front of the class. Have your child come up and take a seat in a chair in front of the class. Next, ask your seated child a simple question such as, "Why didn't you get your homework done for today?" As she answers with a lie, such as "the dog ate my homework," wrap a long string of yarn around her once. Then ask a follow-up question based on her reply, such as "How did the dog get your homework?" As she makes up another answer, wrap the yarn around her again. Continue to ask follow-up questions until she is entangled in a web of yarn. After the class has observed the situation, explain that you asked this person to make up answers to all your questions (to lie). Discuss the following with the class:

1. Ask them if they can see what telling lies can do to someone. Emphasize how one lie usually leads to another and how quickly we can become trapped and embarrassed by lies.

Book Suggestions for Honesty

Kindergarten
Franklin Finders Keepers, Paulette Bourgeois
Berenstain Bears and the Truth, Jan Berenstain
Jamaica's Find, Juanita Havill

First Grade
Arthur's Computer Disaster, Marc Brown
To Tell Truth, Patti Farmer
Sly Fox and the Chicks, Carl Sommer

Second Grade
The Big Fat Enormous Lie, Margorie Weinman Sharmat
Tyrone, The Double, Dirty Rotten Cheater, Hans Wilhelm
Too Many Tamales, Gary Soto

Third Grade
Liar, Liar Pants on Fire, Diane DeGroat
Honest Abe, Edith Kunhardt
Summer Wheels, Eve Bunting

Fourth Grade
Liar, Liar Pants on Fire, Gordon Korman
The Summer When I Was Ten, Pat Brisson
The Honest to Goodness Truth, Patricia C. McKissack

Fifth Grade
If You Had To Choose, What Would You Do?, Sandra McLeod
The Talking Eggs, Robert D. San Souci
The Empty Pot, Demi

2. Ask them what will be experienced by the person who always tells the truth *(not having to remember what your last lie was or how to cover it up, peace of mind, and feeling good about oneself)*.
3. Ask the students to tell about a time when they were caught in a lie and had to tell another lie in order to cover it up.
4. Ask why it is important for us to always tell the truth *(trust, respect, because it's the right thing to do)*.

(*10-Minute Life Lessons for Kids*, Miller)

The Honest Mouth (Suggested for all grades)
Materials: Black licorice

Ask the students if anyone knows what happens when you eat black licorice. *(Put a piece in your mouth—you may want to put extra black food coloring on your piece before visiting the classroom. This will enhance the effect.)* A mouth that has eaten black licorice turns black. *(After chewing, open your mouth to show the result.)* Yuck! Not only does your tongue look horrible, but soon your teeth and even your lips get black. It takes a long time before your mouth returns to its normal color. Dishonesty has a lasting effect on you, just like the black licorice. Just as the licorice leaves our mouths black for a long time, we can see the results of telling lies long after we've told them. Others will lose their trust in us, privileges will be taken away, and friendships will be lost. Telling lies will leave a black ugly mark on you—just like the black licorice. Remember: It's always best to be honest and true; don't let the stain of dishonesty leave its mark on you. (*Object Talks For Any Day*, Kokmeyer)

The Tower of Flour (Suggested for all grades)
Materials: Flour, dime, hard plastic cup, newspaper, butter knife, paper plate

Begin by spreading newspaper on a table. Place the dime in the center of the bottom of the plastic cup. Scoop flour into the glass. Pile it to the brim and press down firmly to make it compact. Place the paper plate on top of the glass and turn them over together on the newspaper. Tap the glass gently, and carefully lift it off. The flour will remain standing in the shape of the glass with the dime on top. Explain that the dime represents the trait *honesty*. Next, take the knife and carefully slice off the edge of the "flour tower," being careful not to cut too deeply. This represents what happened when we tell lies. Our reputation is weakened. Others will not trust or respect us, and eventually the tower of trust falls. Notice how each time more flour is removed the dime's position becomes more precarious. Continue until the dime drops in. (*10-Minute Life Lessons for Kids*, Miller)

Role Play (Suggested for grades 3-5)
Materials: None

Divide the students into small groups. Ask each group to write a short skit to present to the rest of the class in which a person has a choice to be either honest or dishonest. Be sure the students include consequences of the choice in their skit. If you can locate an Abraham Lincoln's hat, you can put skit ideas on strips of paper and have each group select one and act it out.

The Honesty Song (Suggested for grades K-3)
Materials: None

Teach students to sing a song about honesty. They can help them write their own, or you can teach them one like this:
(Sing to the tune of "Yankee Doodle.")

> Honest, honest I will be; truthful and sincere.
> I'll tell the truth and never lie; and will not cheat or steal.
> Honest, honest, I will be; you can count on me.
> I pledge to always tell the truth and answer honestly!

The Honesty Pledge (Suggested for all grades)
Materials: None

Ask the students to write their own honesty pledge. This is the students' promise to always be truthful in their words and actions. After they have finished writing, students can decorate and sign their pledge.

The Cover Up (Suggested for grades 2-5)
Materials: Bucket or large cooking pot (about 8 inches across), one quarter, and enough pennies for each student to have one.

Fill the bucket with 6-8 inches of water and put the quarter at the bottom in the center. Begin by saying that telling a lie may seem like a simple way out of a problem. However, usually when we tell a lie we end up telling even more lies in order to cover up the first lie.*(Give an example, either made up or from your own personal experience.)* Explain to the students that their challenge is to cover up the quarter by using a penny. Have students come up one at a time and try to drop their penny *(from at least 2 inches above the water)* into the bucket and try to cover up the quarter. After everyone has had a turn to drop a penny in the bucket discuss the following questions:

1. How well did the penny cover the quarter?
2. How many actually landed on the quarter?
3. How does this activity compare to trying to cover up a lie that we told?
4. Does someone have to tell more lies to cover up the first lie?
5. What happens when you are caught lying?
6. How easy is it for others to trust you again?
7. Why is telling the truth easier than lying even if the truth may get you in trouble?

(Activities That Teach Family Values, Jackson)

BOOKMARKS FOR HONESTY

"Honesty is always the best policy." —George Washington

"Honesty is always the best policy." —George Washington

"Honesty is always the best policy." —George Washington

"Honesty is always the best policy." —George Washington

"Honesty is always the best policy." —George Washington

"Honesty is always the best policy." —George Washington

"Honesty is always the best policy." —George Washington

"Honesty is always the best policy." —George Washington

"Honesty is always the best policy." —George Washington

"Honesty is always the best policy." —George Washington

(Make copies as needed.)

CARING

Caring

Pre-teach: Tell the students that you are glad to be back today and that you will be discussing this month's trait *caring* with them. Ask the following questions and call on different students for answers. Below each question are examples of the type of responses you are looking for. You may need to rephrase the students' answers or guide them along.

*(Ask) What does it mean to be **caring**?*
1. Showing concern for the well-being of others.
2. Using your words and actions to help someone.
3. Giving of yourself without expecting anything in return.

(Ask) **What are some words that describe the character trait of caring?**
1. Kindness
2. Thoughtfulness
3. Sharing
4. Helping
5. Understanding

(Ask) **What are some ways we can demonstrate caring?**
1. Give to help others in need. For example: collect canned goods for local food pantries, donate gently used clothing and toys, send a card of encouragement to someone who is sick.
2. Show respect to people, property, animals, and the environment.
3. Be kind to everyone and do not exclude others from activities you are doing.
4. Listen to what others have to say.
5. Be helpful in all situations—at school, home and in your community.

(Ask) **Why is it important to be caring towards others?**
1. To make someone else feel better.
2. To help us to feel good about ourselves.
3. To learn compassion for others and to look beyond our own needs.
4. To inspire others to be caring too.
5. To make the world a better place.

Book: Read and discuss a book that teaches a lesson about caring. *(Book suggestions follow.)*

Activity: Complete an activity to go along with your lesson. *(Activity suggestions follow.)*

Closing comment: What's important in life is how we treat each other. At our school, caring is the rule! *(Pass out Caring bookmarks. Bookmarks follow. Make copies as needed.)*

Caring Activities

The Caring Hands

(Suggested for all grades)

Materials: One quarter, a *very* cold empty glass bottle (small soda bottles work great—bring two so you can do the demonstration twice)

Begin by explaining to the class that when people feel lonely or are hurting they may feel cold and sad on the inside, just like your friend here. *(Set your bottle on the table and give it a name. Wet the top of the bottle and place the coin on it, so there are not any gaps.)* But when we reach out to them with caring and kindness, *(place your hands on the bottle to begin warming it)* by using our hands to offer help or to share what we have with them, you can make them feel better. They will most likely show their appreciation and say thank you. Tell the students to listen as your bottle friend wants to say thanks for your caring hands that warmed her up. *(The bottle will make clicking noises as your hands warm the glass, which causes the expanding air to force its way out and push past the coin. The coin drops down with a click after each blip of air. Readjust coin as needed to prevent gaps.)* Helping hands are caring hands!

Waves of Kindness

(Suggested for all grades)

Materials: Beach ball

After you have discussed ways to be caring towards others, explain that one of the nicest things about caring for others is that they're likely to be kind to you in return. Suppose you threw this beach ball into the ocean. The ball would return to you, no matter how hard or far you threw it. The waves would keep rolling in, and before you knew it, the beach ball would come bobbing back to shore. Kind words and action are just like that. You toss them out, and before you know it, someone says or does something to show that he or she cares about you. Caring makes the world a better place for everyone. *(Additional activity: Throw the beach ball to a student, have them share a caring action, and then throw it back to you.)* *(Being Your Best, Lewis)*

Book Suggestions for Caring

Kindergarten
Clifford's Good Deeds, Norman Bidwell
Corduroy, Don Freeman
Swimmy, Leo Lionni
Rainbow Fish to the Rescue, Marcus Pfister

First Grade
Alexander and the Wind-up Mouse, Leo Lionni
Big Al and Shrimpy, Andrew Clements
The Mitten Tree, Candace Christianson
Wilfrid Gordon McDonald Partridge, Mem Fox

Second Grade
A Mother for Choco, Keiko Kasza
Now One Foot, Now The Other, Tomie dePaola
Knots on a Counting Rope, Bill Martin Jr.
The Giving Tree, Shel Silverstein

Third Grade
Angel Child, Dragon Child, Michele Maria Surat
Horton Hears a Who!, Dr. Seuss
Peach and Blue, Sarah Kilborne
Oliver Button Is a Sissy, Tomie dePaola

Fourth Grade
Ferdinand, Munro Leaf
Mufaro's Beautiful Daughters, John Steptoe
More Random Acts of Kindness, Conari Press

Fifth Grade
The Rough-faced Girl, Rafe Martin
Through Grandpa's Eyes, Patricia MacLachlan
Pink and Say, Patricia Polacco

The Color of Caring (Suggested for all grades)
Materials: Two large clear drinking glasses, blue food coloring, bleach

Fill one of the glasses about a quarter full of water. Fill the other glass a little more than half with bleach. Put one or two drops of food coloring into the glass of water. Stir the water to distribute the color. Explain that the blue water represents how someone who is hurting, sad, or lonely might feel on the inside. You've probably all heard the phrase "feeling blue." But when we take the time to be caring and kind to someone who is sad, we can make a difference in their lives. *(Hold up the glass of bleach and say that this represents "caring." Then pour it into the colored water.)* By caring for others, look at the difference we can make in how they feel. Watch as the water slowly starts to turn back to clear. *(While you wait—it will take about a minute—you can discuss ways that we can care for others.)* Clearly, you can make a difference by caring for others!

Cards of Caring (Suggested for all grades)
Materials: None

Have students write notes of appreciation and encouragement to someone in the school (e.g., teachers, the principal, cafeteria workers, office staff, and bus drivers). Arrange with the classroom teacher to have the students personally deliver their caring cards.

The Caring Chair (Suggested for all grades)
Materials: None

Bring a chair up to the front of the classroom and tell the students it will temporarily be known as the "Caring Chair." Invite students to come up one at a time to sit in the chair and give an example of a way to show caring.

Changing The Flavor (Suggested for all grades)
Materials: Two drinking glasses, two cups of fine kitty litter, milk, chocolate milk mix, and two spoons.

The theme of this activity is: Make the world a better place. Explain to the students that milk tastes okay *(hold up a glass of milk)*, but it tastes even better when you turn it into chocolate milk. What if you didn't have chocolate milk mix and you decided to add some kitty litter, because it looks like chocolate milk mix *(stir in spoonfuls of the kitty litter until it looks brownish)*. Ask the class if they think the kitty litter will make the milk taste better. Of course not! To make something better, we have to add the good stuff. Let's get rid of this other stuff and add some of the real chocolate mix to our milk. *(Take the other glass of milk and add the mix.)*. Yum....this is delicious! The same way chocolate can make milk taste better, we can make our world better. When we mix in caring, kindness, compassion, helpfulness, and consideration for others into our world we can make a difference. Remember to add the good flavor of "caring" into our world and make it a better place for everyone. *(Object Talks for Any Day*, Kokmeyer)

The Caring Tree (Suggested for grades K-3)
Materials: Construction paper leaves—at least two for each student

Have each student write a "caring" comment or compliment about another classmate on a leaf. For example: Jill was kind to our new student, or Jack cares for our class when he volunteers to pick up trash. Draw a tree on a large piece of butcher paper or poster board. Have the students take turns reading their leaves and putting them on the tree. To ensure all students are included, you may want to divide the class into small groups and have the group members write a comment for each other. (*The Best of Character*, Hodgin)

Ponder This... (Suggested for grades 3-5)
Materials: None

Write this quote on the board: *"When you are kind to others, it not only changes you, it changes the world."* (Harold Kushner) Discuss with the class the meaning and personal application of this quote in our lives. Next, ask the students to write down an action they can do to show caring and improve the world we live in. Share students' actions with the rest of the class.

BOOKMARKS FOR CARING

"No act of kindness, however small, is ever wasted." —Aesop

"No act of kindness, however small, is ever wasted." —Aesop

"No act of kindness, however small, is ever wasted." —Aesop

"No act of kindness, however small, is ever wasted." —Aesop

"No act of kindness, however small, is ever wasted." —Aesop

"No act of kindness, however small, is ever wasted." —Aesop

"No act of kindness, however small, is ever wasted." —Aesop

"No act of kindness, however small, is ever wasted." —Aesop

"No act of kindness, however small, is ever wasted." —Aesop

(Make copies as needed.)

JUSTICE AND FAIRNESS

CAPTAIN JUSTICE SAYS...

BE COOL,
LET JUSTICE RULE

"LIFE MAY NOT ALWAYS
BE FAIR TO YOU, BUT
YOU CAN ALWAYS BE
FAIR IN LIFE."

Do you seek justice when others are treated unfairly? These people did!

You can be a face of fairness too!

Justice and Fairness

"I know, up on top you are seeing great sights. But down at the bottom we, too, should have some rights."

—Dr. Seuss

Pre-teach: Begin by greeting the students and telling them that you will be discussing the traits *justice* and *fairness* with them today. Ask the following questions and call on different students for answers. Below each question are examples of the type of responses you are looking for. You may need to rephrase students' answers or guide them along.

> *(Ask)* **What is *justice*?**
> 1. Treating everyone fairly under established rules and laws. (You may want to give an example, such as following classroom rules.)
>
> *(Ask)* **What is *fairness*?**
> 1. Treating all people with honesty and respect.
> 2. Giving everyone equal opportunities to succeed.
> 3. Cooperating with one another.
> 4. Celebrating the uniqueness and value of everyone.
> 5. Making sure others are not treated badly.
>
> *(Ask)* **Why are justice and fairness important?**
> 1. To make sure that everyone has the chance to succeed.
> 2. To make our home, school, community, and world better places for all people.
>
> *(Ask)* **Who are some people who have fought for justice and fairness for others?**
> 1. Martin Luther King Jr.
> 2. Rosa Parks
> 3. Abraham Lincoln
> 4. Susan B. Anthony

Book: Read and discuss a story that teaches a lesson about justice and fairness. *(Book suggestions follow.)*

> *(Ask)* **What are ways we can show justice and fairness at our school?**
> 1. Treat all people equally—the same.
> 2. Cooperate with one another.
> 3. Be respectful and listen to what others have to say.
> 4. Be willing to do what is best for everyone.
> 5. Play by the rules at all times; be a good sport.
> 6. Include others in games and activities. Don't leave people out.
> 7. Understand that being fair doesn't always mean the same treatment in every circumstance. For example, you may have an earlier bedtime than your older brother, or your

younger sister may not have as many household chores as you.

8. Stand up for someone you see being treated unfairly—you can make a difference!

Activity: Complete an activity to go along with your lesson. Remember, you can incorporate your activity into your lesson at any time. *(Activity suggestions follow.)*

Closing comment: Life may not always be fair to you, but you can always be fair in life! *(Pass out Justice and Fairness bookmarks. Bookmarks follow. Make copies as needed.)*

Justice & Fairness Activities

Fair Treatment (Suggested for all grades)
Materials: Sack of candy

Bring a sack of candy containing 5 fewer pieces than the total number of students in the class. Pass the sack around and tell everyone they can each take one. When the students discover the unfair situation and that there is not enough candy for everyone, discuss the following questions:

1. How did those students that did not get the candy feel? How about those that did?
2. What would be the fair solution to the problem?
3. Can you think of another situation when people might feel left out or rejected?

You Be The Judge (Suggested for grades 3-5)
Materials: Slips of paper

Before your lesson, write down on slips of paper different "crimes," such as cheating on a test, disobeying a teacher, fighting in the hallway, and stealing a cookie from the cafeteria. Have the students role-play a scene where the "criminal" picks a crime from the hat and the "jury" (the class) decides his sentence. How harsh should the punishment for each crime be? Should the punishment for some crimes be worse than others? Discuss the justice and fairness of the punishments decided by the jury. (*The Best of Character*, Hodgin)

Book Suggestions for Justice and Fairness

Kindergarten
It's My Turn, David Bedford
Miss Spider's Tea Party, David Kirk
The Greedy Python, Richard Buckley

First Grade
It's Not Fair, Carl Sommer
The Doorbell Rang, Pat Hutchins
Jamaica Tag-Along, Juanita Havill

Second Grade
Everett Anderson's Friend, Lucille Clifton
Alexander Who Used to Be Rich Last Sunday, Judith Viorst
Rosa Parks: First Biography, Lola M. Schaefer

Third Grade
Picture Book of Anne Frank, David Adler
The Sneetches, Dr. Seuss
Teammates, David Halberstam

Fourth Grade
Fairness: The Story of Nelly Bly, Spencer Johnson
Minty—The Story of Harriet Tubman, Alan Schroeder
Baseball Saved Us, Ken Mochizuck

Fifth Grade
Fair is Fair—World Folktales of Justice, Sharon Creeden
Picture Book of Sojourner Truth, David Adler
The Cow of No Color, Nina Jaffe

The Fair Eggs-periment (Suggested for all grades)

Materials: Clear drinking glass filled with one cup of water, fresh egg, 1/4 cup salt, a permanent marker, and tablespoon

Carefully place the egg in the glass of water. Tell the students that the egg *(You may want to give it a name like "Eddie")* represents someone who is not being treated fairly. Sinking to the bottom represents how someone who is left out or mistreated would feel—sad, depressed, defeated, unappreciated, and unloved. Remove the egg from the water and set it aside. One tablespoon at a time, add salt to the water. As you stir in each spoonful, explain that the salt represents different ways to show fairness towards others. For example, following the rules when playing a game, taking turns and sharing, treating others with honesty and respect, taking action to help someone being treated unfairly. After you have added all of the salt, put the egg back in the water *(If you want, you can put a smiley face on the egg with the permanent marker)* and it will now float. Explain that now "Eddie" is being supported with kindness and held up by the fairness and acceptance of others. (*10-Minute Life Lessons for Kids*, Miller)

Sing About Justice and Fairness (Suggested for grades K-2)

Materials: None

(Sing to the tune of "You Are My Sunshine")
>   Justice and Fairness, Justice and Fairness,
>   Treat others kindly, respect the rules.
>   Stand up for people who are mistreated,
>   Make a difference in the world.

Fair Cents (Suggested for all grades)

Materials: Ten pennies, two nickels, and one dime.

Stack the pennies on top of one another, stack the nickels next to them, and place the dime beside the nickels. Begin by discussing the fact that although each set of coins looks different, they all have the same value. This is the same with people, we may look different on the outside—short, tall, blonde, etc.—but we are all of equal value and deserve to be treated fairly. When you share, take turns, and treat others equally and with respect, you are showing fairness.

Who Made It? (Suggested for grades 4-5)

Materials: None

Ask the students where they think their clothes are made and by whom. Students may check tags on their own clothing or on the collar of a classmate's shirt. If available, you may want to bring a piece of clothing made in a country with questionable child labor laws (e.g., Pakistan, India, Thailand, Brazil, Mexico, China, and Indonesia). Explain to the students that due to many determined people who took action when they saw injustice by marching the streets in protest in 1908, the United States has laws that protect working conditions and prohibit children from working in factories. Before the workers went on strike, women and children were forced to work in horrible, filthy conditions, for long hours and for very little money. Instead of attending school and playing with friends, young children had to work in factories. Unfortunately, there are still countries in this world that do not have laws that protect children. The children who live in these countries may not have schools or the right to an education. They are expected to work in a factory, perhaps making the very clothes we wear on our backs. Encourage the students to think about ways they can help these children. They may want to check out the following websites with their parents for more information on ways that they can make a difference in the lives of other children living in the world. (www.pbs.org) Resources: www.FreeTheChildren.org; www.Unicefusa.org; www.HistoryPlace:ChildLaborInAmerica.com

Ponder This... (Suggested for grades 4-5)
Materials: None

Write this quote on the board: *"It is not fair to ask of others what you are not willing to do yourself."* (Eleanor Roosevelt) Discuss with the class the meaning of this quote by a former first lady who dedicated her life to improving the quality of people's lives around the world. Have students brainstorm situations they see as unfair and then come up with some solutions together. If time permits, help the class write their own quote about justice and fairness to post in the classroom. For example, "Always be fair and square" —Mrs. Johnson's Class

The Fairness Jar (Suggested for grades 2-5)
Materials: Container and strips of paper

Label a container and place it in a location in the classroom where everyone can reach it. Cut strips of paper and put them in the container. When a student experiences an unfair situation, encourage the student to take out a slip of paper and write a note about what happened and place it back in the jar. Through out the month, ask the classroom teacher to read the notes and talk about ways to make things more fair. (*Being Your Best*, Lewis)

BOOKMARKS FOR JUSTICE AND FAIRNESS

"I know, up on top you are seeing great sights. But down at the bottom we, too, should have some rights." —Dr. Seuss

"I know, up on top you are seeing great sights. But down at the bottom we, too, should have some rights." —Dr. Seuss

"I know, up on top you are seeing great sights. But down at the bottom we, too, should have some rights." —Dr. Seuss

"I know, up on top you are seeing great sights. But down at the bottom we, too, should have some rights." —Dr. Seuss

"I know, up on top you are seeing great sights. But down at the bottom we, too, should have some rights." —Dr. Seuss

"I know, up on top you are seeing great sights. But down at the bottom we, too, should have some rights." —Dr. Seuss

"I know, up on top you are seeing great sights. But down at the bottom we, too, should have some rights." —Dr. Seuss

"I know, up on top you are seeing great sights. But down at the bottom we, too, should have some rights." —Dr. Seuss

"I know, up on top you are seeing great sights. But down at the bottom we, too, should have some rights." —Dr. Seuss

"I know, up on top you are seeing great sights. But down at the bottom we, too, should have some rights." —Dr. Seuss

(Make copies as needed.)

CITIZENSHIP

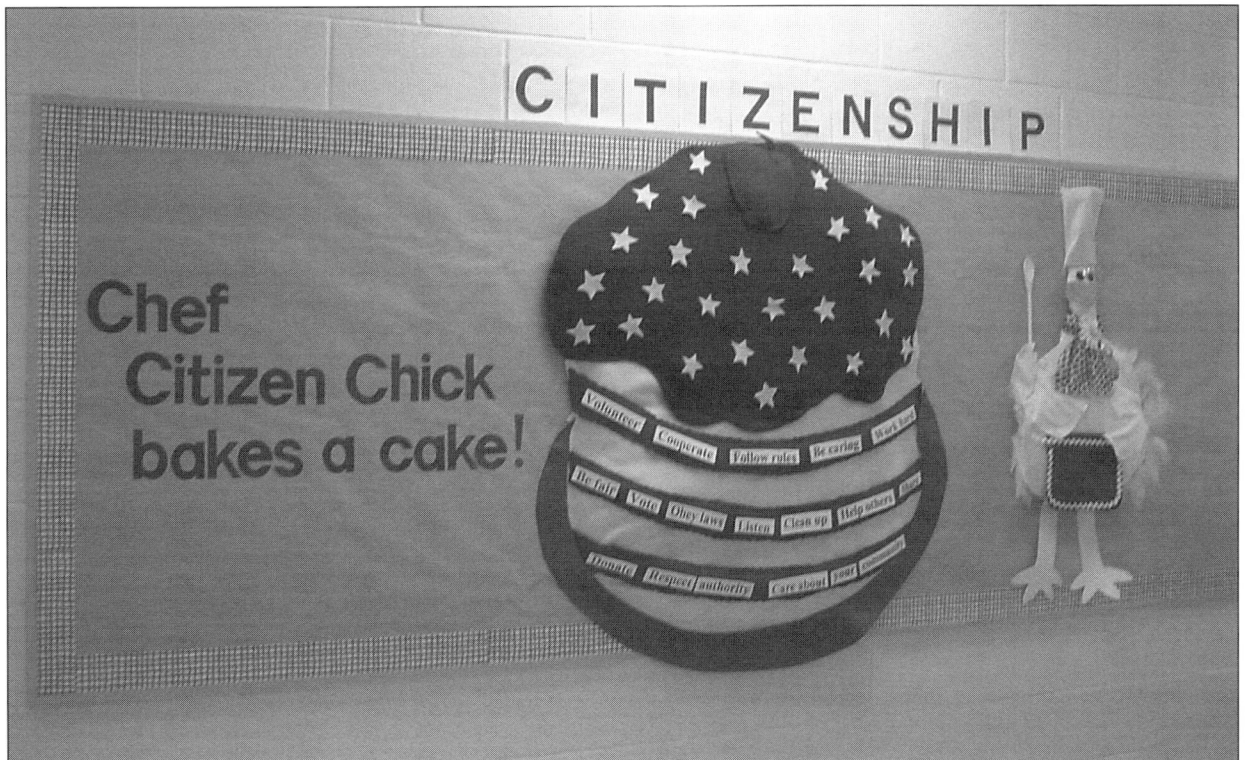

Citizenship

"When all of us work together, we become good citizens and our country becomes stronger."

—Donna Forest

Pre-teach: Greet the students and tell them you will be discussing the character trait *citizenship* with them today. Ask the following questions and call on different students for answers. Below each question are examples of the type of responses you are looking for. You may need to rephrase students' answers or guide them along.

(Ask) **What does *citizenship* mean?**

1. Being responsible and respectful to people, animals, and the environment.
2. Caring about your community and country.
3. Being informed about the needs within your school and community.
4. Doing your best to make your home, school, and community better places.

(Ask) **What are ways you can show good citizenship?**

1. Follow the rules and obey laws at school, home, and in your community.
2. Respect authority (e.g., parents, teachers, police officers, and other community helpers).
3. Participate in activities to improve your community and the environment (e.g., pick up litter, recycle, and plant trees and flowers).
4. Be a good neighbor and volunteer to help others.
5. Donate food or clothing to help someone in need.
6. Learn about the candidates running for public office and participate in youth voting. Encourage others to vote too.
7. Use kind words and good manners in all situations.

(Ask) **Why is citizenship important?**

1. We need good citizens to make our school and community better for everyone
2. It is our duty and obligation as American citizens to do our part.

Book: Read and discuss a book that teaches a lesson about citizenship. *(Book suggestions follow.)*

Activity: Complete an activity to go along with your lesson. You may choose to incorporate an activity at any time during your lesson. *(Activity suggestions follow.)*

(Ask) **What do you think our school and community would be like if people were not good citizens? What if they did not obey rules and respect one another?**

1. Everything would be total chaos! We would not be able learn anything at school, crime would take over in the streets, traffic accidents would be everywhere because people would not follow traffic signals and speed limits, discarded trash and garbage would fill the streets, etc....

(Ask) **Do you think you have the power to make a positive difference in your community?** Yes.

Closing comment: Let's take the Citizenship Pledge: As a citizen, I will care for and respect others. I will take responsibility for improving my community, and I will strive to help my fellow citizens to do the same. *(Pass out Citizenship bookmarks. Bookmarks follow. Make copies as needed.)*

Citizenship Activities

Citizen Ants (Suggested for all grades)
Materials: Chocolate graham cracker crumbs. Chocolate cake sprinkles, zip-lock plastic bags, and plastic spoons

Cooperating and helping one another in order to get something done is a great way to learn about citizenship. Did you know that even the tiniest creatures cooperate with one another? Ants work together to build colonies, gather food, build tunnels, and care for their young. Every ant takes responsibility to perform its special job in order to create a nice ant community to live in. If you would like, you can have the class work together to make an "edible ant farm." Form an assembly line and have group #1 dump graham cracker crumbs into a large bowl. Group #2 can fill sandwich bags half full with crumbs. Group #3 can add a small spoonful of chocolate cake sprinkles "ants" into each bag. Group #4 can zip up the bags. Any remaining students can be responsible for passing out the finished bags and plastic spoons. Conclude your activity by reminding the students that even ants know the importance of citizenship. When we take responsibility to do our part and care for our community, we can make it great! *(Edible Object Talks*, Lingo)

Citizen-tators (Suggested for grades 3 -5)
Materials: You will need a very large potato (Dic*tator*), a very small potato (Commen*tator*), two matching potatoes (Imi*tator*), a potato with large specks on it (Spec*tator*), and a sweet potato.

Book Suggestions for Citizenship

Kindergarten
Franklin Meets the President, Paulette Bourgeois
I Am America, Charles Smith Jr.
Vote for Me! Kirsten Hall

First Grade
Arthur Meets the President, Marc Brown
It Takes a Village, Jane Cowen-Fletcher
A Very Important Day, Maggie Rugg Herold

Second Grade
By the Dawn's Early Light, Steve Kroll
Hawk, I'm Your Brother, Byrd Baylor
Miss Rumphius, Barbara Cooney

Third Grade
America Is..., Louise Borden
The Blue and the Gray, Eve Bunting
Two Days in May, Harriet Peck Taylor

Fourth Grade
John Henry, Julius Lester
Mayor for a Day, Carl Sommer
Sadko and 1000 Paper Cranes, Eleanor Coerr

Fifth Grade
Ballot Box Battle, Emily Arnold McCully
Light Your Candle, Carl Sommer
Dinosaurs to the Rescue, Laurie K. Brown

Explain to the class that citizenship is about taking responsibility to make your community better. The potatoes (or "tators") will show just how different citizens can be. Some citizens are always telling others what to do, instead of helping. This bossy person is called a dic*tator (show large potato)*. Another citizen may not act like a know-it-all, but has a lot of comments to say about everything. They also aren't very helpful. This citizen is a comment-*tator (show small potato)*. Then there are those who only want to do just what everyone else is doing *(show identical potatoes)*. These citizens are imi-*tators*. Just as much a problem are those who wish to only be spec-*tators (show potato with specks)*. Spectators watch everyone else do what needs to be done, but they don't get involved. The sweet potato looks a lot like other potatoes *(hold up the sweet potato)*. But, inside, it is a different color and it has a sweeter taste. A good citizen is like this sweet potato. A good citizen may look the same on the outside, but inside has a "sweet" and kind heart full of respect and concern for others in the community. *(Hold up the potatoes as you talk about them.)* Don't be bossy like the dictator, or all talk and no action, like the commentator. Don't be an imitator, just doing what everyone else is doing, or a spectator that simply watches others work. "Be the sweet potato, full of sweet kindness and concern for your community!" (*Object Talks for Any Day*, Kokmeyer)

Picture This... (Suggested for all grades)
Materials: Pictures and/or stories from a newspaper of local everyday heroes who have demonstrated citizenship

Often a community living section will highlight people who have made a difference in your town. Ask the students to think of other citizens whose actions have made their school or community better.

Citizen Quotes (Suggested for grades 4-5)
Materials: Blank strips of paper and a poster board

Write this quote on the board and discuss what it means: *"You are on the pathway to a successful life when you do more for your community than your community does for you."* (Unknown) Next: Pass out strips of paper and have the students write their own citizenship quotes. Have each student share his/her quote with the class. Glue all of the quotes on a poster board and display them in the classroom.

Recipe for Citizenship (Suggested for all grades)
Materials: Your favorite cookie recipe (cookies for students optional)

Pass out a copy of your favorite cookie recipe to the students. *(You also may want to include a sample cookie for the students to eat while you talk.)* Discuss the ingredients used to make the cookies and the importance of following the recipe to ensure a delicious cookie. Ask the students to consider how the cookies would taste if you didn't follow the recipe. What if you left out the sugar or baked them for too long? Why is it important to follow the recipe? How is this like obeying laws in our community? Ask students to consider what their community would be like without rules and laws. Would it be safe? How do rules benefit our school and neighborhood? Just as we need to follow a recipe to make delicious cookies, good citizens follow and respect the laws at their school and in their community.

The Citizen Chain (Suggested for grades K-2)
Materials: Strips of paper

Cut strips of paper and pass out one to each student. Have them each draw or write a good-citizen action on their strip of paper. Staple the links together and form a "citizen chain" to display in the classroom. Explain that in a community we are all *connected* and must work together to make it a great place to live.

The Citizen Machine (Suggested for grades 3-5)
Materials: None

Ask the students to work in groups of 4-5 to invent a good citizen "machine" (e.g., Acme Trash Collector 1000). Each person in the group must play a part in the function of the machine. Allow students to demonstrate their machine for the class and explain why their machine would be important to the community.

Citizenship Rap (Suggested for grades 3-5)
Materials: None

Teach the students a citizenship rap or have them work in groups to come up with their own. Allow each group to perform their rap for the rest of the class. Sample rap:

> We are good citizens,
> You know it's true.
> We are good citizens in all we do.
> We work hard and respect every rule,
> Helping the community and our school.
> We listen, share and always care,
> We show good citizenship everywhere!

BOOKMARKS FOR CITIZENSHIP

> *"When all of us work together, we become good citizens and our country becomes stronger."*
> **—Donna Forest**

> *"When all of us work together, we become good citizens and our country becomes stronger."*
> **—Donna Forest**

> *"When all of us work together, we become good citizens and our country becomes stronger."*
> **—Donna Forest**

> *"When all of us work together, we become good citizens and our country becomes stronger."*
> **—Donna Forest**

> *"When all of us work together, we become good citizens and our country becomes stronger."*
> **—Donna Forest**

> *"When all of us work together, we become good citizens and our country becomes stronger."*
> **—Donna Forest**

> *"When all of us work together, we become good citizens and our country becomes stronger."*
> **—Donna Forest**

> *"When all of us work together, we become good citizens and our country becomes stronger."*
> **—Donna Forest**

> *"When all of us work together, we become good citizens and our country becomes stronger."*
> **—Donna Forest**

> *"When all of us work together, we become good citizens and our country becomes stronger."*
> **—Donna Forest**

(Make copies as needed.)

COURAGE

COURAGE

Stand up for what is right,
even if you stand alone.

Courage

"Courage conquers all things."
—Ovid

Pre-teach: Greet the students and tell them that today you will be discussing the trait *courage*. Ask the following questions and call on different students for answers. Listed below each question are examples of the types of responses you are looking for. You may need to rephrase students' answers or guide them along.

> *(Ask)* **What does *courage* mean?**
> 1. Doing the right thing even if it is difficult.
> 2. Facing your fears with confidence—being brave.

> *(Ask)* **What are some ways you can show courage?**
> 1. Do the right thing, even if others are not.
> 2. Bravely deal with your daily challenges.
> 3. Be willing to try new things, even if you might fail.
> 4. Tell the truth regardless of the consequences.
> 5. Face your fears and work to overcome them.
> 6. Admit your mistakes and learn from them.
> 7. Do not give into negative peer pressure

> *(Ask)* **Can you name some people who have shown courage?**
> 1. Rosa Parks, Martin Luther King, Susan B. Anthony, soldiers, police officers, fire fighters

Book: Read and a discuss story that teaches a lessons about the trait courage. *(Book suggestions follow.)*

> *(Ask)* **Which action is courageous and which is foolish?**
> 1. Fighting, or walking away from a fight?
> 2. Doing something dangerous that others are doing, or not participating even if someone calls you "chicken?"
> 3. Teasing and bullying someone, or standing up for someone who is being mistreated?
> 4. Blaming others for your mistakes, or accepting responsibility?
> 5. Ignoring a new student, or making friends with a new student?
> 6. Only looking out for yourself, or helping others?
> 7. Following the crowd, or doing what's right?
> 8. Quitting when things get tough, or working hard, even when it's difficult?

Activity: Complete an activity to go along with your lessons. *(Activity suggestions follow.)* Remember, you can incorporate your activity at any time during your lesson.

Closing comment: It takes courage to do the right thing. Stand up for what is right, even if you stand alone. *(Pass out Courage bookmarks. Bookmarks follow. Make copies as needed.)*

Courage Activities

The Courageous Egg
(Suggested for all grades)

Materials: Wide-mouthed glass or jar, uncooked rice, egg

Place the egg in the middle of the glass completely covered by rice. Explain that the egg represents someone who hanging with the crowd. One day the group starts making fun of other people. The egg doesn't like it so he tells them to stop. *(Tap the top of the rim, the egg will rise up from the rice with each tap.)* Next, the group of friends starts excluding others from their games *(tap the rim)* and they start telling lies. Each time the egg refuses to go along with his friends and stands up for what's right *(tap again)*. Continue until the egg has completely risen above the rice. Tell the students it takes courage to do the right thing when others are not. A courageous person will rise to the top and stand out from the rest!

Book Suggestions for Courage

Kindergarten
The Brave Little Bird, Scott Beck
Rainbow Fish to the Rescue, Marcus Pfister
Brave Irene, William Steig

First Grade
Nessa's Fish, Nancy Luenn
There's a Monster Under My Bed, James Howe
Brave Potatoes, Toby Speed

Second Grade
The Bravest Dog Ever, The True Story of Balto, Natalie Standiford
Dogzilla, Dav Pilkey
Pets to the Rescue, Andrew Clements

Third Grade
The Children's Book of Virtues, William Bennett
The Boy Who Held Back the Sea, Thomas Locker
Brave as a Mountain, Ann Herbert Scott

Fourth Grade
The Children's Book of Heroes, William Bennett, ed.
Chicken Soup for Kids, Stories of Courage, Jack Canfield
Saint George and the Dragon, Margaret Hoages

Fifth Grade
The Big Wave, Pearl Buck
Kids with Courage, Barbara Leaks
Secret of the Peaceful Warrior, Dan Millman

The Courage to be Different (Suggested for all grades)
Materials: Food or clothing from a different culture

Share the food or clothing with the class. Encourage them to try the food or have someone put on the clothing. Discuss that it takes courage to try something new or wear clothes that are different from what others are wearing. Talk about how it takes courage to do many things in life, like making friends with a new student or admitting a mistake. Ask the students to share examples of their own acts of courage.

On a Roll (Suggested for all grades)
Materials: One sheet of copy paper, small book

Show the class the piece of paper and ask them if there is any way the paper can hold up the book, using only one hand to hold the paper. You can ask for several volunteers to try, soon they will realize there is no way. Now take the paper and roll it tightly into a tube, the diameter of about 1 to 1/2 inches. Hold the tube in one hand and carefully place the book on top of the open end of the tube. It should support the book. Relate this to the ability we all have to turn our weaknesses into strengths and show courage. The paper at first is flimsy, weak, lacking backbone and character—it's easy to crush and overwhelm. This might be compared to some people who are faced with a problem or obstacle; they may lack the courage to confront the problem or stand up to the opposition. But with determination, we can turn our weaknesses into strengths. Just as the paper can be rolled into a sturdy tube, we can work to add muscle to our weaknesses if we have the courage to persist. We will then develop backbone to hold up under pressure. Ask the students to give examples of what someone could do to turn a weakness into strength. Examples: Marty has to give a presentation in class and he is afraid to speak in front of his classmates. Jackie loves to play basketball but she is short for her age. She is afraid to sign up for the team because her skills might not measure up. (*10-Minute Life Lessons for Kids*, Miller)

Act It Out! (Suggested for grades 3-5)
Materials: None

Have students work in small groups to role-play situations in which a person shows courage. You may want to write possible scenarios on note cards and distribute one to each group. Allow each group to perform its skit for the rest of the class. Remind students to be a respectful while others are performing.

Gone Fishin' (Suggested for all grades)
Materials: Paper, hole punch, paper clips, wooden dowel, string, magnet, and a can,

Give each student a small piece of paper. Have them fold it in half. On the upper half, have them write down something they are, or were, afraid of. On the lower half, have them write what they did or can do to get over this fear. They do not need to put their name on the paper. Punch a hole through the top of both pieces of paper near the fold, then attach a paper clip. Have students place the pieces of paper in a can. Give students a "fishing pole"—a wooden dowel with string and a magnet attached to the end. Have the students take turns dropping the end of the pole into the can. The magnet will attach to the paper clip. Then students "reel in" the clip of paper and read what is on the paper. Discuss how it takes courage to overcome our fears. (*The Best of Character*, Hodgin)

What Does Courage Look Like? (Suggested for all grades)
Materials: Drawing paper

Have students draw a picture of courage in action. Have them title their pictures by completing the sentence "Courage is..." If possible, display the pictures in the classroom.

A Quote To Ponder (Suggested for grades 3-5)
Materials: None

Write this quote on the board and discuss it with the students: *"Courage is being scared to death...and saddling up anyway."* (John Wayne) Next, ask the students to write and illustrate their own quote for courage. Display them in the classroom.

BOOKMARKS FOR COURAGE

"Courage conquers all things."   —Ovid

"Courage conquers all things."   —Ovid

"Courage conquers all things."   —Ovid

"Courage conquers all things."   —Ovid

"Courage conquers all things."   —Ovid

"Courage conquers all things."   —Ovid

"Courage conquers all things."   —Ovid

"Courage conquers all things."   —Ovid

"Courage conquers all things."   —Ovid

"Courage conquers all things."   —Ovid

(Make copies as needed.)

PERSEVERANCE

IT TAKES PERSEVERANCE TO FULFILL YOUR DREAMS

"Be like a postage stamp, stick to something until you get there."
—JOSH BILLINGS

PERSEVERANCE

37 USA

Perseverance

"Never, never, never give up!"
—Winston Churchill

Pre-teach: Greet the students and tell them that today you will be discussing the trait *perseverance*. Ask the following questions and call on different students for answers. Listed below each question are examples of responses you are looking for. You may need to rephrase students' answers or guide them along.

(Ask) **What is *perseverance*?**
1. Staying with the task and not giving up.
2. Showing commitment, pride and a positive attitude in completing tasks.
3. Trying again and again and again.
4. Being patient and willing to work hard.

(Ask) **Can you name some people who have shown perseverance?**
1. Lance Armstrong, Thomas Edison, Harriet Tubman, Helen Keller, Stevie Wonder, etc.

"Be like a postage stamp— stick to something until you get there!"

—Josh Billings

Book: Read and discuss a story that teaches a lesson on perseverance. *(Book suggestions follow.)*

(Ask) **What are ways you can show perseverance?**
1. When you are near the end of race and struggling to finish, find a burst of energy to cross the finish line.
2. Try a new sport or skill that is difficult and keep working at it.
3. Study and work hard to improve your grades.
4. Save up your money and do extra chores to buy something special.
5. Help a younger child learn to ride a bicycle or play a new game.
6. Spend hours practicing to play an instrument.
7. Always finish what you start. Do not give up when things get tough.
8. Try something again, even if you failed the first time. Remember you had to learn to walk before you could run!

Activity: Complete an activity to go along with your lesson. *(Activity suggestions are follow.)* You can incorporate your activity at any time during your lesson.

Closing comment: It takes perseverance to fulfill your dreams. *(Pass out Perseverance bookmarks. Bookmarks attached. Make copies as needed.)*

Perseverance Activities

Icy Perseverance (Suggested for grades 2-5)
Materials: An ice cube for each student with a penny frozen inside

Begin your lesson by giving each student an ice cube. Explain that the first person to get the penny out of their ice *without* putting it in their mouth or hitting it with another object is the winner. You may want to continue your lesson until you have a winner. Afterwards discuss:

1. How does melting the ice cube compare to reaching your goals?
2. Did you ever feel like quitting? Why do some people quit before reaching their goals?
3. Could you have gotten the penny quicker had you broken the rules? Would you feel as good about winning if you didn't follow the rules?
4. How do hard work and perseverance help you achieve your goals?

Sink or Swim? (Suggested for grades K-3)
Materials: Clear glass bowl with water, modeling clay (not Play-Doh)

Roll clay into four balls, three of them small and one a little larger (like small and big marbles). Drop each small one into the water and watch them sink. Tell the students that each ball represents a person that feels discouraged or frustrated by life's difficulties. We all feel like that at times. Just like the clay balls, you may want to give up and sink into a sad state of despair. *(You can give the clay balls pretend names and talk about why each one might be feeling low. For example, Susie is struggling to finish her science project on time and wants to give up...)* Next, take the larger clay ball and start reshaping it to form the shape of a simple canoe. Talk about how this person is not going to give up when faced with a problem. He or she is choosing to have a positive attitude and show perseverance. Discuss how it's possible to work through the challenges and achieve your goal by "reshaping" your attitude. Put the "boat" in the water and watch it float. Now take each small ball and put them inside the boat. Ask the students what can happen when a person has a positive attitude and decides to persevere. They not only achieve their goal, but are a positive role model for others. (*10-Minute Life Lessons for Kids*, Miller)

Book Suggestions for Perseverance

Kindergarten
The Little Engine That Could, Watty Piper
The Very Busy Spider, Eric Carle
The Carrot Seed, Ruth Kraus

First Grade
Are You My Mother?, P.D. Eastman
The Itsy Bitsy Spider, Iza Trapani
Turtle's Race with Beaver, Joseph Bruchac

Second Grade
Princesses Are Not Quitters, Kate Lum
The Tortoise and the Hare, Janet Stevens
Wanda's Rose, Pat Brisson

Third Grade
Flossie and the Fox, Pat McKissack,
I Have a Dream, Margaret Davidson
Perseverance: The Story of Thomas Alva Edison, Peter Murray

Fourth Grade
Amazing Grace, Mary Hoffman
More than Anything Else, Marie Bradby
Addy Saves the Day, Connie Rose Porter

Fifth Grade
Wilma Unlimited, Kathleen Krull
Fly, Eagle, Fly, Desmond Tutu
I Knew You Could, Watty Piper

All Shook Up! (Suggested for grades K-2)

Materials: Three or four plastic jars with tight lids, a plastic bowl, three or four pints of whipping cream, honey, plastic knives, and sliced bread

Pour a pint of whipping cream into each container and place the lids on securely. Pass the jars among the students, giving each student a moment to shake the jar before passing it on. Remind them not to give up...with perseverance they will have delicious butter. While the students are shaking the jars, you may want to read a story. After a few minutes of shaking, stop the students and ask them what would happen if they gave up now. Explain that quitting keeps great things from happening. If we lose patience and give up, nothing good will develop. It should take about 10 minutes for the cream to separate into a lump of butter in each jar. Carefully remove the butter and place it in a large plastic bowl. Drizzle honey over the butter. Invite the kids to spread the delicious treat on a piece of bread. Perseverance is a "sweet" character trait to generously spread throughout our lives! (*Edible Objects Talks*, Lingo)

Reach for the Stars (Suggested for all grades)

Materials: Paper stars

Give each student a paper star. Have them each write a dream or goal that they hope to achieve on their star and then decorate it. Tell the students that it takes perseverance to fulfill their dreams.

Act It Out! (Suggested for grades 3-5)

Materials: None

Have students work in small groups to write their own skit demonstrating perseverance. Allow each group to present to the class. This activity may require a little more time, so check with your classroom teacher in advance.

Hands of Perseverance (Suggested for grades 3-5)

Materials: Copies of sign language alphabet

Obtain a copy of the sign language alphabet from the library or the internet. Make copies and handout to the students. Using the handout, teach the students to spell out the word perseverance as you discuss what it means. Then ask the students to spell out words that represent perseverance. For example: focus, determination, positive, sure, and goal. (*The Best of Character*, Hodgin)

Try, Try, Try Again!! (Suggested for grades 2-5)

Materials: None

Discuss this quote from Thomas Edison: "I never failed once when I invented the light bulb. It just happened to be a 2,000-step process." Consider how different life might be today if Mr. Edison had chosen to quit after his first few attempts to invent the light bulb. Have the students work in pairs or small groups to write their own quote for perseverance, and then share their quotes with the class.

I Think I Can, I Think I Can... (Suggested for grades K-1)

Materials: Story of "The Little Engine That Could"

After reading *The Little Engine That Could* have students form a long train, with you being the conductor. While you lead the train around the room have the students repeat the phrase "I think I can, I think I can..." Remind the students that with perseverance they *can do anything*!

Stick to It! (Suggested for grades K-3)

Materials: Empty paper towel tubes, enough for each student to have one

Give each student a paper towel tube and explain that they will make a perseverance stick. Have students write the words "Stick to it!" on their tube and then decorate it. Explain to the students that they are to take the stick home. When they see a friend or family member show perseverance, they are to write that person's name on the stick. Encourage students to share with their family the names of people they saw showing perseverance. *(You may want to bring a sample completed stick with you and talk about how you used it.)*

BOOKMARKS FOR PERSEVERANCE

"Never, never, never give up!" —**Winston Churchill**

"Never, never, never give up!" —**Winston Churchill**

"Never, never, never give up!" —**Winston Churchill**

"Never, never, never give up!" —**Winston Churchill**

"Never, never, never give up!" —**Winston Churchill**

"Never, never, never give up!" —**Winston Churchill**

"Never, never, never give up!" —**Winston Churchill**

"Never, never, never give up!" —**Winston Churchill**

"Never, never, never give up!" —**Winston Churchill**

"Never, never, never give up!" —**Winston Churchill**

(Make copies as needed.)

HOPE

Hope

Pre-teach: Greet the students and tell them that today you will be discussing the trait *hope*. Ask the following questions and call on different students for answers. Listed below each question are examples of the type of responses you are looking for. You may need to rephrase the students' answers or guide them along.

> *(Ask)* **What does it mean to have hope?**
> 1. Believing you will be successful.
> 2. Believing what you desire is possible.
> 3. Being optimistic and positive about your future.

> *(Ask)* **How can we demonstrate hope in our lives?**
> 1. Having a positive attitude, even when facing difficult situations.
> 2. Being willing to work hard and always doing your best.
> 3. Pursuing your goals and following your dreams.
> 4. Helping and encouraging others when they are down.
> 5. Practicing your faith.

> *(Ask)* **Who are some people we know that show hope?**
> 1. Your parents, grandparents, school teachers and staff
> 2. Friends or family members who are dealing with illness or a difficult situation
> 3. Helen Keller, Henry Ford, Anne Frank, Martin Luther King Jr., Thomas Edison, Harriet Tubman, Mother Teresa, and others

Book: Read and discuss a story that teaches a lesson about the trait hope. *(Book suggestions follow.)*

Activity: Complete an activity to go along with your lesson. *(Activity suggestions follow.)* You can incorporate your activity into the lesson at any time

Closing comment: (Read the poem below and pass out Hope bookmarks. Bookmarks follow. Make copies as needed.)

> Hope is believing your dreams will come true,
> It's knowing you'll be successful in all that you do.
> You will need to work hard and have patience too,
> But when you have *hope* each day is brand new.

> **Have hope for your tomorrow!**

Hope Activities

Lighten Up! (Suggested for all grades)
Materials: Dark sunglasses

If possible, begin by entering the classroom wearing the sunglasses. Exclaim that it is really dark in here. Everything is so dark, even the walls, desks and students look dark. I wonder why that is? *(Someone will likely state that you have on dark glasses.)* Your response: Oh, I guess that's true. I don't really need glasses in here. I just left them on because it was easier than taking them off. That may sound kind of silly, but have you ever known someone who talked as if they *always* had on dark glasses? Someone who always looks on the dark side of everything isn't much fun to be around. Instead of being happy with the sunshine, she is worried because it might rain tomorrow. Instead of being glad to be at school, he is stressed about an upcoming assignment or whether or not he will win the game. For some people, it's easier to be unhappy than it is to be happy. If you are like that, it's time to work on being more hopeful. We demonstrate the character trait of hope by keeping a positive outlook and believing that we will be successful. Don't let problems keep you from the joy hope can bring, not only to yourself, but to others around you. Don't look on the dark side of life *(put on your glasses, then take them off again as you continue),* lighten up and be a ray of hope and sunshine to everyone around you! *(Object Talks for Any Day,* Kokmeyer

Act It Out! (Suggested for grades 3-5)
Materials: None

Have the students work in small groups and role-play situations where they demonstrate giving hope to others. Examples of some situations: a student does poorly on a test, someone has to move away, a student has a mom who is sick, another student may be afraid to give a speech in class, a student who did not make the team. Have the groups each act out their situations in front of the class. Fourth and fifth graders might also enjoy discussing the meaning of the following quote from an unknown author: *"When the world says 'Give up!' hope whispers, 'Try it one more time.'"*

Listen Up! (Suggested for grades 3-5)
Materials: CDs of recent kids' music, CD player

Check into the music kids are listening to lately and find examples of optimistic and hopeful lyrics and those without them. Bring the music in and play it for the class. Have the students

---

Book Suggestions for Hope

Kindergarten
A Chair for My Mother, Vera B. Williams

First Grade
I Hope You Dance, Mark D. Sanders

Second Grade
Owl Moon, Jane Yolen

Third Grade
Song of the Swallows, Leo Politi

Fourth Grade
Tree of Hope, Amy LittleSugar

Fifth Grade
Chicken Soup for the Soul: Stories of Hope, Jack Canfield

---

listen to and discuss the lyrics. Determine whether or not they offer a message of hope. Discuss how words in the music can influence our thoughts and actions.

The Top Ten Reasons for Hope Are... (Suggested for grades 2-5)
Materials: Poster board, marker

Work together as a class and come up with ten top reasons why it is best to have hope. Consider putting them on a poster board and displaying them in the classroom.
Example: Our Top Ten Reasons for Hope Are...

    1. It makes you a stronger person.
    2. You help and encourage others.
    3. You will accomplish more in life.

(*Teaching Character*, Dotson and Wisont)

Do What The Sunflowers Do (Suggested for grades K-2)
Materials: A paper plate, scissors, crayons or markers, green construction paper and Popsicle sticks

Referring to the Helen Keller quote, have students decorate a paper plate to look like a sunflower and then attach it to a Popsicle stick. The students can cut out small leaves to glue on the sides of the Popsicle stick.

BOOKMARKS FOR HOPE

"Keep your face to the sunshine and you cannot see the shadow. It's what the sunflowers do."
—Helen Keller

"Keep your face to the sunshine and you cannot see the shadow. It's what the sunflowers do."
—Helen Keller

"Keep your face to the sunshine and you cannot see the shadow. It's what the sunflowers do."
—Helen Keller

"Keep your face to the sunshine and you cannot see the shadow. It's what the sunflowers do."
—Helen Keller

"Keep your face to the sunshine and you cannot see the shadow. It's what the sunflowers do."
—Helen Keller

"Keep your face to the sunshine and you cannot see the shadow. It's what the sunflowers do."
—Helen Keller

"Keep your face to the sunshine and you cannot see the shadow. It's what the sunflowers do."
—Helen Keller

"Keep your face to the sunshine and you cannot see the shadow. It's what the sunflowers do."
—Helen Keller

"Keep your face to the sunshine and you cannot see the shadow. It's what the sunflowers do."
—Helen Keller

"Keep your face to the sunshine and you cannot see the shadow. It's what the sunflowers do."
—Helen Keller

(Make copies as needed.)

PARENT LETTERS

BUILDING CHARACTER

RESPECT

Dear Parents,

We not only want our students to have strong minds, but also strong morals. This is why each month throughout the school year, we highlight a different character trait. We would like to pass along some ways you can further discuss the trait at home with your family. Let's face it, as parents we are our children's greatest influence. That's why when it comes to building good character...*there's no place like home!*

RESPECT AT HOME

1. After a family meal, take turns having family members share something they respect and appreciate about each other. Next, you may want to think about extended family, friends, and neighbors and the qualities they have that you appreciate.

2. Take a cup full of uncooked rice and dump it on a plate. Then ask family members to take turns retrieving each grain using chopsticks. Compare this difficult task with "picking up" unkind words that have spilled from our mouths.

3. Establish a no "put-down" policy in your home. For example: Anyone who says something unkind to another family member must make that person's bed!

4. On the next trip to the grocery store with your child take the opportunity to point out ways to show respect to others. While waiting in line, let someone with fewer items go ahead of you or allow someone who has been waiting longer than you to move over to the check-out lane that just opened. Be polite to the cashier and take your cart back to the corral when you are finished. Explain to your child that actions like these show that we value and respect others and their property.

THE GOLDEN RULE:

Always treat others as you would like them to treat you.

The Rewards of Respect

- We develop effective social skills and habits.
- We make other people feel good.
- We earn the respect of others.
- We establish good relationships.
- We are treated better by other people.
- We improve our feelings of self worth.
- We build a solid reputation.

**from *Life's Greatest Lessons:
20 Things that Matter* by Hal Urban**

"100 years after you die it won't matter what car you drove or what house you lived in. But it will matter how you raised your kids."

A bumper sticker in Charlotte, NC

BUILDING CHARACTER...THERE'S NO PLACE LIKE HOME!

BUILDING CHARACTER

RESPONSIBILITY

During an interview, the employer said to the applicant, "In this particular job, it's very important that we hire someone who is responsible." The applicant replied, "Then I'm the one you want. In my last job, every time something went wrong, they said I was responsible!" Well, none of us wants our children to grow up to be like this unfortunate job applicant. This is why we start teaching our children at a very young age the importance of responsibility. Hopefully, this month's newsletter will give you some new thoughts on teaching this valuable trait in your home.

RESPONSIBILITY AT HOME

1. Establish a "Work Then Play" household rule.

2. Be a role model. Let your children see you being accountable, organized, prepared, and on time.

3. Volunteer together. "Community service increases social responsibility and a sense of personal competence," according to John Rutledge, 4-H youth development specialist of family, youth, and community sciences.

4. Use a shopping trip as a way to teach a lesson in financial responsibility. Bring along a calculator and have your child add up his/her desired items. How much allowance money would it take to make his purchase? The goal is to help your child appreciate the cost of food and the value of a dollar.

5. Create an action plan for ways your family can be more environmentally responsible. For example: recycle more, turn off lights, limit water consumption, carpool, etc.

Allow your children to make choices, and let them know that they must accept the outcomes. From an early age, expect them to make regular, tangible contributions to the family. That means chores they don't get paid for. And it means letting your children take responsibility for their own actions.

from _Parenting 101_ by John Rosemond

"If you want your children to keep their feet on the ground, put some responsibility on their shoulders."

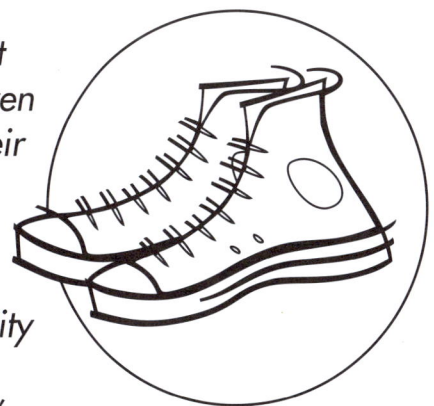

Abigail Van Buren

BUILDING CHARACTER...THERE'S NO PLACE LIKE HOME!

BUILDING CHARACTER

HONESTY

One day, a 4-year-old named Justin came running out of the bathroom to tell his mom that he'd dropped his toothbrush in the toilet. His mom fished it out and threw it in the trash. Justin stood there thinking for a moment, then ran to his mother's bathroom and came out with her toothbrush. He held it up and said with a smile, "We better throw this one out too then, 'cause it fell in the toilet a few days ago." Honesty, how sweet it is! Inspire your family to practice honesty every day.

HONESTY AT HOME

1. Be honest in everything you say and do. Avoid any of those "little white lies."

2. Establish an Honesty Honor Roll for the month of November—a special way to recognize family members' honesty in action.

3. Play the George Washington Game. Ask your child to tell about a time he had been tempted to be dishonest. Discuss the positive consequences of telling the truth and the negative ones had he chosen to lie (e.g., guilt, loss of respect and privileges, punishment, embarrassment). Afterwards, share a similar situation that you have faced.

4. Look for truth and honesty in advertising. Tune in on Saturday morning with your child and watch a few commercials of the latest toys being marketed to kids. Help your child discern what she is seeing. Is the toy really as big and fun to play with as the advertiser makes it seem?

5. Check out the newspaper to find examples of honest and dishonest actions to share with your child. Discuss possible reasons why people lie, cheat, or steal, and the consequences of their decisions.

What if...
(A situation to discuss)

Your older sister has a fancy, expensive watch she bought with money she earned babysitting. She lets you wear the watch to school for a party. Your friends think it's your watch, and they're impressed. They gather around you and look at you with wide eyes. Someone says, "You must be rich to have a watch like that." You know you're not rich, but it feels good to have everyone think so. What will happen if you tell the truth? If you don't? Does it matter in a case like this? Why or why not?

from *Being Your Best* by Barbara Lewis

"Don't worry that your children never listen to you; worry that they are always watching you."

Robert Fulghum, author

BUILDING CHARACTER...THERE'S NO PLACE LIKE HOME!

BUILDING CHARACTER

CARING

Need for Speed Underground for Playstation 2: $49
Bratz Tokyo-A-Go-Go Collection: $39
Digital camera with 5.0 megapixels: $279
Time spent listening and showing genuine concern
for one another: Priceless.

This holiday season consider acts of caring and kindness for your gift list.
HAPPY HOLIDAYS!

CARING AT HOME

1. Play the "Caring Game." Write down on strips of paper at least 15 actions that show caring. (For example: give someone in the family a hug, or help with the laundry.) Fold the papers in half and place them in a bowl. Sit in a circle and place a bottle in the center. Select a member of the group to spin the bottle. When the bottle stops, have the person the bottle is pointing to pick a slip of paper and complete the action written on the paper, either right then or at a later time. Each person keeps the slips of paper they select.

2. Using a soft indoor ball, take turns throwing the ball back and forth to one another. Each time you throw the ball you give the person you throw it to a compliment. Point out something that is special about him/her.

3. Make "caring" cards for family, friends, and community helpers. Let these folks know how much they are appreciated. Help the kids deliver the cards with a smile.

20 Gifts to Give

1. Mend a quarrel.
2. Seek out a forgotten friend.
3. Hug someone tightly and whisper, "I love you so."
4. Forgive an enemy.
5. Be gentle and patient with an angry person.
6. Express appreciation.
7. Gladden the heart of a child.
8. Find the time to keep a promise.
9. Make or bake something for someone else— anonymously.
10. Speak kindly to a stranger.
11. Enter into another's sorrow.
12. Smile. Laugh a little. Laugh a little more.
13. Take a walk with a friend.
14. Kneel down and pat a dog.
15. Lessen your demands on others.
16. Apologize if you were wrong.
17. Turn off the television and talk.
18. Thank someone who helped when you hurt.
19. Give a soft answer even though you feel strongly.
20. Encourage an older person.

from *The Finishing Touch* by Charles Swindoll

"The power of love and caring can change the world."

James Autry

BUILDING CHARACTER...THERE'S NO PLACE LIKE HOME!

BUILDING CHARACTER

Justice & Fairness

If your house is anything like mine then the phrase, "That's not fair!" is uttered by children more often than you'd like. Sometimes their concern is legitimate and sometimes it's not. However, when we take the time to talk it out and help them work through situations at home, we give them the confidence they'll need to speak up for themselves and for others when treated unfairly. Just like it says in the poem "Children Learn What They Live" by Dorothy Law Nolte, "If children live with fairness, they learn justice."

JUSTICE & FAIRNESS AT HOME

1. Establish your own "Family Court." Invite family members to fill out a "complaint" form when they experience a situation they feel is unfair and place it in a designated box or envelope. One a week read and discuss all of the concerns together. Talk about ways to make things more fair for everyone.

2. Play a simple game. Take two crumbled tissues and put them side by side at the end of a long table. Next, see who can blow his paper to the other end first. Comment on your child's reaction when he either wins or loses. Use the opportunity to talk about playing fair and being a good sport.

FOUR WAYS to Treat People Fairly

Find ways to share, take turns, and feel less jealous.

Ask people what you can do to help make things more fair

Include others in games and activities. Don't leave people out.

Respect people who are different from you.

Being Your Best, Barbara Lewis

People with Character

- They walk with integrity.
- They do what is right.
- They tell the truth.
- They don't gossip.
- They don't mistreat people.
- They side with those who are right.
- They keep their word.
- They lend money to those in need without interest.
- They don't take advantage of people for financial gain.

from A Diamond in the Rough by Andrew Stanley

"The sun shines upon all alike."

English Proverb

BUILDING CHARACTER...THERE'S NO PLACE LIKE HOME!

BUILDING CHARACTER

CITIZENSHIP

I recently saw a bumper sticker that read "Giving makes living better." People who have discovered this truth know that life is more meaningful when you give to others. Good citizens are willing to reach out, listen up, respect all, and give unselfishly in the home and community, and around the world. This month as we talk about citizenship, challenge your child to find a way to serve others and make a difference in your home and community.

CITIZENSHIP AT HOME

1. Discuss ways you can show citizenship at home and consider a weekly "Good Citizen" award for the best effort. (For example: Cleaning up without being told, helping a sibling with homework, letting someone else be first, etc.)

2. Initiate a neighborhood clean-up. Take a trash bag and go for a walk in your neighborhood. Pick up all of the discarded trash along the way. Good exercise and community service all in one!

3. To demonstrate to your child how doing her part and working together is important, have her and a friend make a sandwich together. Give them each one slice of bread and allow each one to use only one hand. The bread can not be folded and must be cut to make the sandwich. It can be a little messy, but should give them a taste of citizenship.

Imagine what our neighborhood would be like if each of us offered just one kind word to another person. There have been so many stories about the lack of courtesy, the impatience of today's world, road rage, and even restaurant rage. Sometimes, all it takes is one kind word to nourish another person. Think of the ripple effect that can be created when we nourish someone. One kind empathetic word has a wonderful way of turning into many.

**from *The World According to Mister Rogers*
by Fred Rogers**

"I am only one, but still I am one. I cannot do everything, but still I can do something; I will not refuse to do the something I can do."

Helen Keller

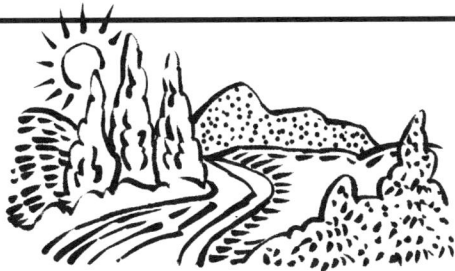

"You are on the pathway to a successful life when you do more for your community than your community does for you."

Anonymous

BUILDING CHARACTER...THERE'S NO PLACE LIKE HOME!

COURAGE

BUILDING CHARACTER

Two seeds lay side by side in the fertile spring soil. The first seed said, "I want to grow! I want to send roots deep into the soil beneath me, and push my sprouts through the earth above me. I want to unfurl my tender buds like banners to announce spring. I want to feel the warmth of the sun on my face and the fresh morning dew on my petals." And so she grew. The second seed said, "I am afraid. If I send my roots into the ground below, I don't know what I will encounter in the dark. If I push my way through the hard soil above me I may damage my delicate sprouts. What if I let my buds open and a snail tries to eat them? And if I were to open my blossoms, a small child may pull me up from the ground. No, it is much better for me to wait until it is safe." And so she waited. A yard hen scratching around in the early spring ground for food found the waiting seed and promptly ate it. (*Chicken Soup for the Soul*, Hansen) Moral of this story: Without the courage to try new things in order to grow, you will be swallowed up by life.

COURAGE AT HOME

1. Create a "Badge of Courage" to bestow on family members who demonstrate courage when facing a difficult situation.

2. Inspire your child to show courage by sharing a story about a hero. Look for examples from your family history or the newspaper.

3. Role-play situations with your child by asking questions such as, "How would you practice courage if your friends want you to try something that you know is wrong, or you are playing with a toy you borrowed and it breaks?" Talking through possible real-life dilemmas beforehand gives your child confidence to do the right thing.

4. Celebrate courage by deciding as a family on a challenge that requires courage...then do it together (e.g., introduce yourselves to a new neighbor or an old neighbor you don't know).

Actions that Take Courage

• Admitting you are wrong.
• Doing what is right when everyone else isn't.
• Speaking to someone you don't know.
• Saying "no" when people are trying to get you to do something you know you shouldn't do.
• Telling the truth and accepting the consequences.
• Standing up for something you believe in even though it may mean rejection or ridicule.
• Confronting a fear without running away.
• Defending someone who is unpopular.
• Being the only one.
• Taking a risk.
• Sharing your heart honestly.

Dr. Steve Stephens, psychologist

Courage is not the towering oak
That sees storms come and go,
It is the fragile blossom
That opens in the snow.

Alice MacKenzie Swaim

BUILDING CHARACTER...THERE'S NO PLACE LIKE HOME!

BUILDING CHARACTER

PERSEVERANCE

Some of the greatest success stories of today are of people who have persevered in spite of great obstacles. Walt Disney was fired from his job as a newspaper editor because he lacked creative ideas. He later filed bankruptcy several times and was told repeatedly to forget the "mouse idea" because there was no future in it. Three-time Olympic gold medal winner Wilma Rudolph was crippled as a young child after contracting polio. She was told she would never walk again. Instead of giving up, she *ran* and became known as the "Fastest Woman in the World." Success is about not giving up when the going gets tough. It's persevering through life's trials and tribulations until you reach your goal. This month as we focus on the trait perseverance, consider sharing some of your own personal success stories with your children. Inspire them to keep reaching for the stars and to never give up.

PERSEVERANCE AT HOME

1. In the spirit of baseball legend Babe Ruth's perseverance (hitting 714 home runs in spite of 1330 strike outs), use a baseball and write the initials of family members on it when they show perseverance.

2. Bounce a ball back and forth with your child to illustrate the importance of "bouncing back" after she encounters a setback or failure in life. Encourage your child to learn from her mistakes and grow stronger from them. "It's not whether or not you get knocked down. It's whether you get back up again." —Ralph Waldo Emerson

3. Watch the movie "The Journey of Natty Gann" (Walt Disney, 1985) with your family. It is a story told during the Great Depression of the 1930s about a young girl's journey to join her father, who is logging in the Pacific Northwest. It is a story of perseverance, courage, and hope. "Homeward Bound" is another entertaining family movie about perseverance.

The Miracle Bridge

The Brooklyn Bridge that spans the river between Manhattan and Brooklyn is simply an engineering miracle. In 1869, a creative engineer, John Roebling, was inspired by an idea for this spectacular bridge project. However, bridge-building experts told him it just was not possible. Roebling convinced his son, Washington, an engineer, how it could be accomplished, and how to overcome the obstacles. Somehow they convinced bankers to finance the project and with great excitement hired their crew to begin to build their dream bridge.

The project was only a few months under way when a tragic on-site accident killed John Roebling. Washington continued with the project until he developed a terrible illness from continuously working underwater. He was bedridden and unable to walk or talk. Everyone thought that the project would be scrapped since the Roeblings were the only ones who understood how the bridge could be built.

Though Washington Roebling was not able to speak, his mind was as sharp as ever. One day, as he lay in his hospital bed, an idea flashed in his mind as how to develop a communication code. All he could move was one finger, so he touched his wife's arm with that finger. He tapped out the code to communicate to her what she was to tell the engineers who continued building the bridge. For 13 years Washington communicated his instructions through his wife until the spectacular Brooklyn Bridge was finally completed in 1883.

Adapted from *A Fresh Packet of Sower's Seeds* by Brian Cavanough

"The greatest oak tree was once a little nut who held its ground."

Author Unknown

BUILDING CHARACTER...THERE'S NO PLACE LIKE HOME!

HOPE

BUILDING CHARACTER

Imagine living in a world without hope—a place where no one believes they can succeed or dream about their tomorrow. This month as we focus on the character trait *hope*, we will teach students that their dreams are possible with hard work, perseverance and a positive attitude. In addition to focusing on having hope in their own lives, we will also learn about the importance of giving hope and encouragement to others, of being a light in the darkness.

HOPE AT HOME

1. Listen to the lyrics of your child's favorite songs. Determine whether or not they are words of encouragement and hope, or messages of despair and hopelessness. Talk about them with your child and discuss how words in music can influence our thoughts and actions. Encourage your child to turn off the negative influences and tune into the positive ones.

2. During a family meal have everyone at the table share something they have really hoped for. It may be as simple as a certain gift or a passing grade on a test to something as involved as healing for an ill loved one or peace in Iraq. Either way, discuss how in each situation that family member demonstrated hope. If it is something yet to happen then talk about ways to continue to keep their hope alive.

3. Have your child name at least three things that he/she can do to inspire hope and encouragement in a brother, sister, or friend who may be struggling with a difficult situation.

If we do not teach our children hope, then who will dream for a better tomorrow? The ups and downs of life are much easier to take when we believe that what we desire is possible and that we have the power to make a difference.

Thank you for taking the time this school year to read these monthly letters and follow through in your home with character development. You are giving your child a gift of character that will last a lifetime.

"Learn from yesterday, live for today, hope for tomorrow."

Author Unknown

BUILDING CHARACTER...THERE'S NO PLACE LIKE HOME!

SURVEY

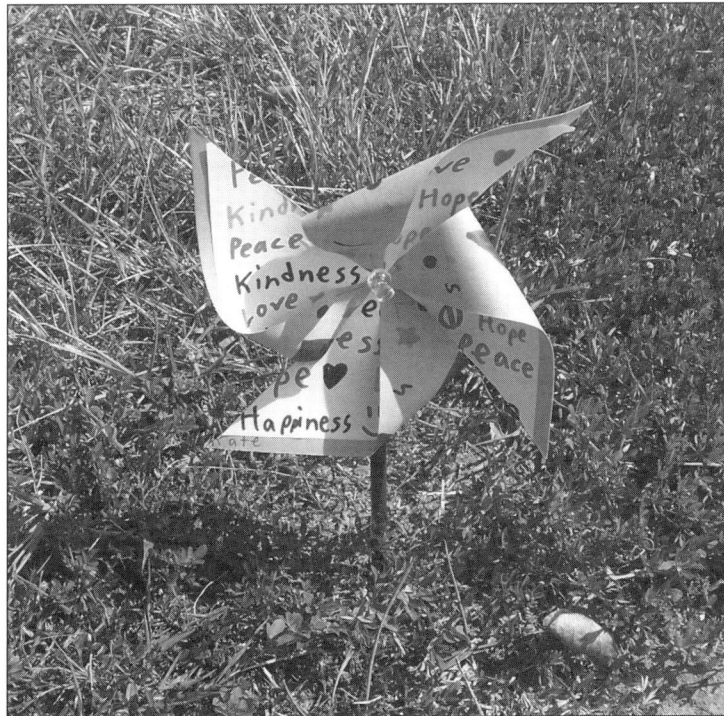

Character Education Volunteer Monthly Survey

Teacher/Grade: _____

Date of presentation: _____

Book title: _____

Discussion: _____

_____

_____

Activity: _____

_____

Student response: _____

_____

_____

Is there anything you would change next time? _____

_____

_____

Thank you for completing this form. Please leave it in the envelope marked "Survey" on the character education bookshelf.

CHARACTER SKITS

The Kitchen Band

(A Little Ditty About Respect)

Adapted from *The Skit Book*

Cast: Any number of players, a band director

Action: Players come on stage in a dignified manner carrying an assortment of kitchen items: pots, pans, egg beaters, wooden spoons, mixing bowls, etc. With much ado, the director tunes them up. They begin to play on their instruments to a silly tune, made-up song or the school song. They can even sing along; some may be off-key.

Ending: Have one of the cafeteria staff storm onto the stage and take back the utensils. She should exclaim loudly, "Hey, I can't prepare lunch without my cooking utensils. You need to learn to *respect* other people's property!" The musicians apologize. Then one steps forward and says, "Remember, it's important always to show respect to others *and* their property. Treat other people the way you would want to be treated." The musicians bow and exit the stage.

Do the Right Thing

Cast: A small group of 3 or 4 people. A person sitting alone

Scene: A park

Action: The person sitting alone is reading a book. The group of people walk by talking and laughing together. As they pass, a wallet drops out of a pocket and onto the ground. No one in the group notices and they keep on walking. The person reading sees the wallet and walks over to pick it up, looking around to see if anyone else is watching. There is no one else in the park. Then the person opens the wallet and comments on all of the money inside. The person exclaims, "I could really use this money to buy that new skateboard I've been wanting. (smiling) I guess it's finders keepers, losers weepers." Then the person stops and thinks for a moment. "But wait, even though no one else knows about this wallet, keeping it just wouldn't be right. I could never feel good about it. Besides, honesty is always the best policy.

Ending: The person runs offstage shouting, "Hey, wait a minute! You dropped something!" Then all of the cast members come back on stage arm in arm, and one person says, "Having good character means doing the right thing even when no one else is looking!"

The Operation

(A Lesson in Perseverance)

Adapted from *The Skit Book*

Cast: Doctor, nurse, and a patient

Scene: An operating room, A patient is on the table, covered by a sheet.

Action: The nurse announces that the famous surgeon, Dr. Rocket, is about to operate. The doctor comes on stage with much fanfare and begins to operate. The doctor pretends to pull out a series of absurd items from the patient's stomach (e.g., a jump rope, a toilet plunger, a globe, a cell phone, etc.). Each time the doctor exclaims, "Oh, I see the trouble now," but there is always one more to pull out.

Ending: Finally, the doctor pulls out something very, very tiny (like a marble) and exclaims, "Oh, here's the trouble! It took perseverance, but this patient will be just fine. Nurse, remember always to commit to your goals and never ever give up! Persevere!" While the doctor is speaking, he/she puts everything else back in and sews the patient up.

Fishing for Responsibility

Cast: A fish, its owner, and a sign person

Scene: The fish bowl

Action: The sign person holds up a sign that says "Day One." The fish has just been brought home from the store by its new owner and placed in the fish bowl. *(The fish character should move all around and pretend to flap its gills excitedly and make fish faces.)* The fish exclaims, "Wow, my very own room. It's so nice and clean. My new owner seems so excited to have a new pet!" Sign person steps forward and holds up the next sign: "Day Two." The fish swims around looking a little worried and exclaims, "I wonder where my new owner is. I'm really hungry and kind of lonely." Sign person holds up the sign "Day Three." Now the fish is swimming slower and looking very sad. The fish says, "I haven't seen my new owner since she brought me home from the store. I'm so hungry and lonely. She promised her mom she would take *responsibility* and care for me and keep me company every day. Oh wait, here she comes! Hello friend, I've missed you! Thanks for the food. Please don't go so soon..." Sign person holds up sign: "Day 27." The fish is swimming very slowly and looking very sad. "My fish bowl is so dirty I can barely see out and my water is filthy. My owner only occasionally drops some food in my bowl, but never changes my water or spends any time with me. *(crying)* I'm so sad! I miss my friends at the pet store! I don't think I can take this much longer."

Ending: Sign person steps forward and says, "See what can happen if we don't follow through on our responsibilities? It's important always to keep your promises and do what is expected of you. Others are depending on you! Remember: Only *you* have the ability to have *responsibility*." The sign person puts her arm around the fish and walks her off stage saying,"Don't worry little fishy, you can come home with me and I'll take good care of you. I'll feed you every day, change your water weekly, spend time with you..."

A Friend in Need Is a Friend Indeed

(Caring for Others)

Cast: A group of friends and a new student

Scene: On the playground

Action: The scene begins with the friends talking and *(pretend)* playing basketball together. The new student is off to the side sitting by herself. Someone in the group starts to talk about the new student, making fun of the fact that she is very tall. The new student is obviously self-conscious and feeling very sad and lonely. One student in the group steps forward and tells the others to stop saying mean and hurtful things about the new student. The student goes on to tell the others that the new student is really very nice if they would just get to know her. Also, because of her height she would make a great basketball player for their team. She then goes over to the new student, talks with her and invites her to play basketball with the rest of the group. The student exclaims, "Thanks for caring enough to be my friend."

Ending: The caring student introduces the new student to the rest of the kids. The others change their attitude and realize their friend was right. They all proceed to play basketball together and treat the new student warmly. The caring student steps forward (holding the basketball) and says, "Caring for others is contagious...pass it on!" (She passes the ball to another student.)

The Spellbound Citizens

(The Importance of Citizenship)

Adapted from *The Skit Book*

Cast: Eleven letter carriers and a spelling director

Action: All letter carriers come on stage, each holding a sign with a different letter from the word "citizenship." *(Have some lively music playing in the background.)* The letter carriers mill about trying to form a word. They form the wrong word at first, shake their heads and try again. Eventually the spelling director comes on stage to help them. She begins to arrange the letters in the appropriate order. Some letters may have their own personalities and not want to stay in place, others may get tired and lie down, etc.

Ending: The spelling director finally gets all of the letters in place and they spell out the word "citizenship." The spelling director steps forward and says, "It is important for each of us to remember that we all have a responsibility to work together and make our community a better place. Here are some ways you can be a good citizen." The spelling director calls out each letter. As the letter is called, the holder turns around to show the other side of the sign revealing an action—for example: vote, recycle, etc. "When we each do our part, great things can happen! That's what citizenship is all about!"

A Sign of Courage

Cast: A large group (about 8-10 people), and one courageous person

Action: The group slowly walks *(with solemn expressions)* in a single file line from the back of the room, through the audience and toward the stage. Each person is carrying a sign with a different action on it (e.g., stealing, lying, teasing, cheating, fighting, hating, etc.). The last person in the group is carrying a sign that reads "follower" as she follows the group to the stage. Before reaching the stage she stops and turns toward the audience. The group also stops and turns to look at her. She exclaims, "This is wrong, very wrong. I am not just going to follow the crowd. I am going to have *courage* and follow *my* conscience instead." She puts down the sign she is carrying and picks up another that reads "courage." "I am going to do the right thing, even if others *(gestures to the group)* are not!"

Ending: The courageous person smiles bravely and proceeds toward the back of the room through the audience. One at a time, the group members look at the courageous person, put down their signs *(smiling)*, pick up a "courage" sign, and follow her out of the room.

Fairness Rules

Cast: A group of about 5 friends (Two should have brown hair/brown eyes.)

Scene: Happyland Amusement Park

Action: The skit begins with the friends walking on stage toward the park entrance. They are talking excitedly about the fun they will have at the park. As they approach the entrance they stop to read a sign. One person in the group steps forward and reads the sign out loud. "Only people with brown hair and brown eyes are allowed to enter Happyland Park. No exceptions!" She turns around and faces the rest of her friends and exclaims, "I can't believe it! That means only two of us can go into Happyland. The rest are not allowed just because of the color of our hair and eyes. That's not fair!" One of the brunette friends walks toward the entrance and exclaims, "Well, it won't be as fun without you guys, but I've been looking forward to going to Happyland and I'm not going to miss out! *(She motions to her other brown-haired friend.)* Come on, let's go in." Her friend shakes her head and exclaims, "No way, it is not right for Happyland to treat people differently just because of the color of their eyes or hair. People should *never* judge others based on the color of their hair, eyes, skin or *anything* else. It's about *fairness* and giving the same treatment to everyone. Happyland's rule is wrong and we should not support it by going in and leaving our friends behind."

Ending: The first brunette walks back to the group and says, "You're right. I'm so sorry. I just got carried away with the excitement of going to the park." Another friend exclaims, "Why don't we all go back to my house and write a letter complaining about the unfair rule to the president of Happyland. We can even send a copy to the newspaper. Maybe together we can make a difference." The friends all agree and walk back across the stage. Someone in the group says, "I think they are building a new park that should open soon. It's going to be called Rocketland—the place where fairness rules!"

BIBLIOGRAPHY

Bertolini, Rebecca. *Mom's Big Activity Book for Building Little Characters* (Wheaton, Ill.: Victor Books, 1992).

Dotson, Anne C. and Karen D. Dotson. *Teaching Character: Teacher's Idea Book* (Chapel Hill, N.C.: Character Development Group, 1997).

Graham, Leland and Isabelle McCoy. *Character Education: The Ladder to Success* (Greensboro, N.C.: Carson-Dellosa Publishing, 2004).

Hodgin, Duane. *The Best of Character* (Chattanooga, Tenn.: National Center for Youth Issues, 2001).

Jackson, Tom. *Activities That Teach Family Values* (Cedar City, Utah: Red Rock Publishing, 1998).

Kokmeyer, Verna. *Object Talks for Any Day* (Cincinnati, Ohio: Standard Publishing, 2001).

Lewis, Barbara A. *Being Your Best* (Minneapolis, Minn.: Free Spirit Publishing, 2000).

Lingo, Susan L. *Edible Object Talks that Teach about Values* (Cincinnati, Ohio: Standard Publishing, 2000).

McDonald, Margaret. *The Skit Book* (Hamden, Conn.: Linnet Books, 1990).

Miller, Jamie. *10-Minute Life Lessons for Kids* (New York: HarperCollins Publishers, 1998).

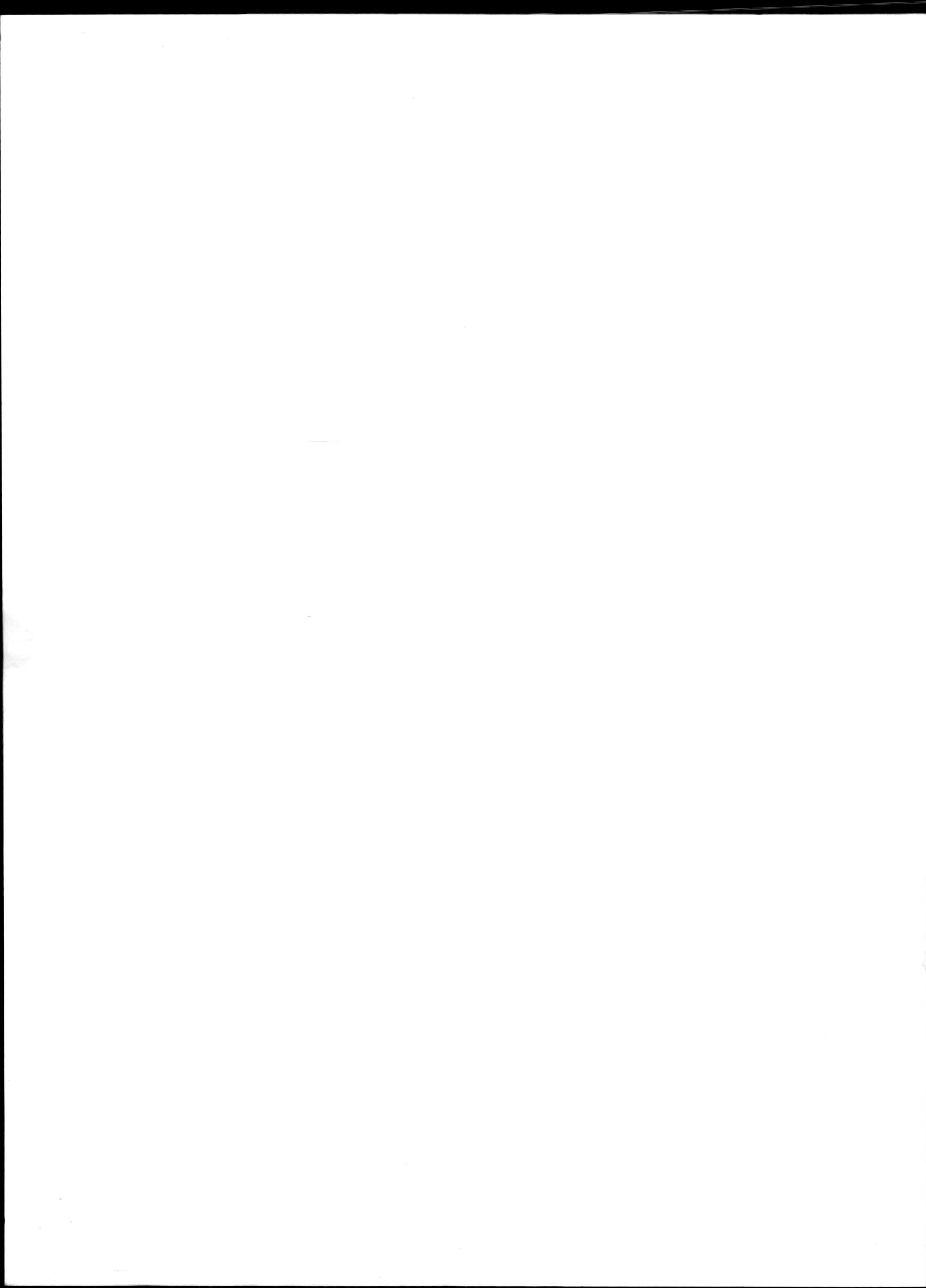